CARNON 1
BACKALONG
by E.J.Irwin

Dick Jennings shoeing
Photo by Jack Green

First published 2005
by Landfall Publications
Landfall, Penpol, Devoran, Truro, Cornwall TR3 6NR
in association with Carnon Downs Local History Group:
A. Appleby, Jenny Burrows, John Crowe, David Griffith,
Jean Lapham, David and Catherine Lobb, Mary Rudd,
all of whom I thank for their contributions.

ISBN 1 873443 51 X

A CIP catalogue record for this book is available from the British
Library.

Printed by the Troutbeck Press
and bound by R Booth Ltd, Antron Hill, Mabe, Penryn, Cornwall

Dedicated to Arthur, who put up with his wife drifting into another
century and forgetting his supper, and who spent weeks measuring
and building for the exhibition in October 2004.

Above: Treliever from Grenna Lane
Below: The Carnon Viaduct from Carnon Wollas

Abbreviations within

Background reading

We read and recommend
> Books by Hamilton Jenkin, who read hundreds of Victorian reports and journals about Cornwall and listened in the 20th century to personal tales from the century before
> Richard Carew's *Survey of Cornwall*. He died in 1620.
> Letters from Celia Fiennes, who travelled through Cornwall on horseback in 1628
> Workbooks of Feock Parish Local History Group and their books published in 1972
> Books by Bob and Viv Acton
> *Agricultural Hand Tools* by Roy Brigden
> *Horse-drawn Farm Machinery* by D.J. Smith
> *House on a Heath*, about Carnon Downs Chapel, E.J.Irwin 2003

Vivid insights come also from
> Extracts from 19th century *West Briton*
> Articles from journals e.g. Cornwall Association of Local Historians, Old Cornwall Society, Cornwall Polytechnic Society, Government Commissions on Agriculture and Mining
> Minutes of Feock Parish Vestry and early days of Parish Council
> Deeds of Carnon Downs houses
> People who listened to their grandparents
> Walking rights of way
> History of Carnon Downs chapel, the centre of learning, discipline and celebration from 1825

Contents

Acknowledgements

We have relied on encouraging guidance through
a maze of information from staff of
Cornwall Record Office
Redruth Cornish Studies Library
Courtney Library, Royal Institution, River Street
and from Bob Acton, Barry Simpson, Christine North,
and the memories of many. It is a communal effort.
Financial help came from Local Heritage Initiative,
without whom we would not have dared to begin.

Local Heritage *initiative*

PLOTS BEFORE PLANNING
PEOPLE BEFORE PLUMBING

The aim of this book is to discover what Carnon Downs was before 1900, that is before concrete housing, internal combustion engines and mains supplies.

The first stimulus to such curiosity was the Feock Parish History group's study led by Veronica Chesher and published in 1972. It is out of print but a few treasured copies are in private hands and in the Courtney Library. The second was the exhibition about Carnon Downs arranged by Jean Lapham in the Methodist hall in 2000. Both of these deserve to be preserved and available, especially since major changes to roads and buildings have happened so fast that only a few families remember the place back to the 1920s and the rest of us are newcomers with roots somewhere else.

We have concentrated on the 19th century because there is so much information hidden away. What houses there were can be counted on the 1842 tithe map. Who lived here is listed in censuses; some surnames occur many times and no addresses are given so matching occupants to houses involves some best guessing. In the Record Office there are musty parchments about leases in the 18th and 19th centuries, and there are wills and surviving parts of Feock births, marriages and deaths registers. The Courtney Library has books and maps and unpublished research work. The Redruth Cornish Studies Library has books and journals. All of these institutions are staffed by patient archivists who point the way. Some householders have deeds for their plots, and the big sales in the 1920s describe fields and houses one by one. Rights of way are a clue because they must have been trodden for a purpose. Even trees in hedges suggest the age of boundaries. So do the shape and size of fields on Ordnance Survey large scale maps of about 1880: small square fields are usually 18th and 19th century enclosures while large curved and irregular field edges may belong to older estates.

Wander through the village, in your hand an old map of scale 1:10,000 if you can find one, and see in your imagination the scattered settlements and the families within. Wonder where was the nearest water, what did they eat, how did they keep warm and clean, how travel, what skills were needed for employment and who provided for the elderly and destitute. How did a wild heath become the green pastures and pretty gardens of today?

WHAT WAS CARNON DOWNS?
WHICH OF THE FOLLOWING ARE TRUE?

It was a burial site.

It claims no Celtic saint of its own.

It was wasteland not recorded in Domesday.

It was a crossroads before there were houses.

It was on a main road from Helston to London in 1497 when Michael Joseph, rebelling against taxes, marched through.

Old Carnon Hill was part of the Turnpike Trust from Truro to Penryn and Helston from the mid-18th century.

To the east is the good farmland of Feock. To the west and south were mineshafts, tips, engine houses, stamps, chemical works.

When the price of copper slumped there was employment in farming. When the price of wheat slumped there was rural poverty.

Here was built the first Christian church in the parish since Feock church, on land leased from Lord Falmouth.

Tenants enclosed heath bit by bit, cultivated it with only hand tools, and carried sand and manure and seaweed on the backs of small horses and donkeys.

Ore-carrying donkeys rested in the fields.

The land was so improved that it grows hay and oats, flowers and fruit, and supports horses and cattle.

A potato patch and a pig were necessities to make ends meet.

There were claypits and quarries for building houses.

Enterprising craftsmen here were shoemakers, smiths, carpenters, masons.

GOOD OLD DAYS
by David Griffith

Today it is hard to imagine living in a Victorian small-holding with no running water in the house, no sewage system, no gas or electricity and consequently no refrigerators, cookers, quick light and heat, or any other gadget requiring power.

For example, half the week could be taken up with laundry. Monday was wash day, unless it was Tuesday because clothes had to be soaked all Monday to loosen the grime. Mother's first job, probably before breakfast, was to light the wash boiler fire. If you were lucky the wash house was near the cottage, otherwise you dodged the rain to the top of the garden. Clothes had to be boiled in the copper, so called although it was usually cast iron, as soap was expensive and scarce until 1880.

Considerable physical effort was needed to manipulate the dolly, the fore-runner of the washing machine in its action. A preparation called lye, which you made by pouring rain water through wood ash, was often used. Another aid to dislodge the dirt was a washboard, this also needing physical effort. I met a lady in the 1990s who still 'streamed' her clothes in the Lamorna valley.

All the water had to be carried in buckets from the well, in your own garden if you were lucky, but it might be from a communal well down the road. A stream at the bottom was a bonus. Drying the clothes was a problem so ironing day was when the laundry was dry enough. It was hung outside on fine days and finished off round the fire especially in winter. Not all the homes had a mangle. Some villagers had a 'bleaching green' where laundry was laid out in the sun; bushes were also used.

There were many types of iron, the simplest a flat or sad iron which was heated on the range. In 1830 it cost 1/-. These were box irons, heated by a metal slug called a boxheater which was hooked red hot out of the fire. These cost 3/-. There were coal irons, charcoal irons, and brass-bottomed irons, a luxury for ironing delicate fabrics. A 'Mrs Potts' iron had a detachable wooden handle which did not get hot while on the range, and a set of three bases.

While all this was going on hens had to be fed, also perhaps a pig, vegetables tended, bread baked, rats, mice and bugs eliminated and meals cooked. Men were not expected to do any housework. If they had to, because the wife was ill or heavily pregnant, they often locked the door as domestic chores were considered effeminate. Children from about 5 until they went out to work at 10 did little but look after their siblings in the large families which were normal.

Worn out at the end of the day the poorest families went to bed early especially in winter. When the fire had died down and there was no more light bed was the only option. Although it was possible to make your own candles, if you had the knowledge and the facilities, they were expensive. It was possible to make rushlights but these needed constant attention and one of the children had the job of constantly trimming the wick. A cruise lamp, fuelled by skimmings of the bacon pot, was the cause of many a house being burnt down, and candles were not much safer. Parents often had a box bed downstairs and early in the century children climbed a ladder to sleep under the thatch which often leaked rain water. A stone or a brick was heated by the fire to warm the bed. Oil lamps became popular and within reach of most pockets in the middle of the 19th century.

You may think I have exaggerated how primitive life was in Victorian times, but as a boy in the late 1920s and '30s I experienced almost everything I have written here. Father did no housework but worked hard in the garden and our plates were piled high with vegetables in season: peas, beans, carrots, onions, leeks, celery and spinach in summer, brussels, cabbage, cauliflower, kale and turnips in winter. I can still see my father, before church on Sunday, sitting shelling a colander full of peas for the four of us. As a result, at teatime I had butter on my bread as well as jam, but many of my contemporaries at the village school had either but not both. Fifty years before they would have had bread alone.

Going back to Victorian times, I have ignored landowners, whose life was so different it was like another world. Professional families too could employ servants and were spared the privations. Farmers, tradesmen, craftsmen, were able to improve their lot, but even these when ill or old were dependent on their offspring.

EVEN OLDER DAYS

Before history began, maybe 3000 years ago, Carnon Downs had tumuli. These are shown on Ordnance Survey maps in a field south of Park Farm, at 50 Knights Meadow, in Parc-an-creeg, in Killiganoon. The name 'Gear' of a field at Tregye may mean a prehistoric camp.

The Domesday book written in 1086 records:

'Godwine holds LANDIGEA (Landighe). Alsige held it TRE and it paid geld for 1 virgate of land. Yet there is one hide. There is land for 5 ploughs. There are 1½ ploughs and 5 slaves and 2 villans and 4 bordars and 2 acres of meadow and 3 acres of woodland. There is pasture 1 league long and as much broad. Formerly 50s now worth 10s.

'Richard holds GOODERN (Woderon). Alwine held it TRE and it paid geld for 1 virgate of land. Yet there is half a hide. There is land for 3 ploughs and 2 slaves and 2 villans and 4 bordars and 6 acres of woodland. There is pasture 5 leagues long and 1 league broad. Formerly 20s now worth 10s.'

These are translations of the entries about the two manors nearest to Carnon Downs. TRE means in the time of King Edward. A hide in Cornwall is about 120 acres, a plough is the area that can be ploughed by one 8-ox team in a year, a league is 1½ miles. Villans, bordars, slaves, are the male inhabitants not counting their families, and the worth of the land is the tax taken by the king. The whole of Cornwall was owned by William the Conqueror and under him by the Bishop of Exeter and churches, and by the Count of Mortain, William's half-brother, who was rewarded after the battle of Hastings with 277 manors out of the county's 340. Most of these he handed to powerful men who were expected to support him in war, such as Godwine and Richard Fitzturold. As for Alsige and Alwine, they were dispossessed.

Between the cultivated patches was at least as much of wild land, a source of timber and furze, picked over by men searching for tin as for instance was Carrine Common. Carnon Downs is not mentioned and presumably was also wild.

At the time of Henry VII a different system of land tenancy was replacing manors: land was leased to tenants for a term of years, often 99, but limited to the lifetime of the last of 3 named people who were usually a man, wife and child, but could be any 3 relations. The lease was bought and rent was paid. Ownership of land was by wealthy men who acquired it by pleasing the king and by marrying heiresses and by good management and industry.

Sir William Lemon was born poor, worked in a Chacewater coppermine, managed Chyandour smelting house, invested his money and his wife's in mines including Poldice, and becoming rich bought Carclew. He died in 1760 and his descendants bought good farmland on both sides of Old Carnon Hill and along the Carnon River.

The Boscawen family of Tregothnan acquired tracts of land on the west side of Old Carnon Hill including the 31 acres of heath called 'Carnon Downs'.

The Agar-Robartes of Lanhydrock owned land at the bottom of Old Carnon Hill continuous with Devoran.

A description of Cornwall was published in the *St James Chronicle* in 1776: 'The whole face of the country is rudely furrowed, turned over by thousands of miners. The west end is subject to heavy, cloudy, rainy weather so that people obliged to be much abroad are wet to the skin and over shoes in dirt. The natives seem happy when they can sit down to a furze blaze wringing their shirts and pouring mud and water out of their boots. 'Labourers bring up their families with potatoes and turnips or leeks or pepper grass rolled in black barley crust and baked under ashes. Yet their children are strong and look fresh and jolly.'

How did the 'rudely furrowed' ground of slate, quartz and clay become by 1900 the pattern of lush grass and hawthorn, holly and oak hedges, with scattered slate and cob houses and wide stony tracks, some of which we still see today?

Luckily some of the Lemon estate documents are safely kept in the Cornwall Record Office and the history of the Lemon properties can partly be followed. The documents, some sealed with red wax, are written with ink on parchment which is stiff with age, each one about 60x60 cm folded into a square the size of a lady's handkerchief, requiring some force to unfold and to hold flat, powdery with yellow dust, patchily stained orange. Some of the writing is legible but because the lines are so close and 60 cm long it is difficult for the eye to follow from one line to the next. The language is strange, beginning with a respectful note of the monarch and the year of his reign, and listing names 'of the first part', 'of the second part', and describing 'that messuage lately occupied by ...' or 'a moiety of that tenement'. It is repetitious and lacks punctuation. It is hard to discover who is leasing what to whom. It is thrilling however to imagine a clerk inscribing in the reign of Queen Anne or George III, and to witness the signatures of people who made their homes in this village and nearby two centuries ago. It is like wandering into a dream.

WHAT THE VICTORIANS DID IN CARNON DOWNS
The clearest way to start is with the tithe map of 1842. To see the real thing ask at the Cornwall Record Office. On the copy here you can recognise roads and houses. From the censuses can be compiled lists of residents and sometimes their occupations. Because no addresses are given in the censuses,and because some surnames occur many times, not all the houses and people can be perfectly matched.

Imagine the village with only the houses on the tithe map, among arable fields and hedges, with rights of way to wells and streams and with patches of waste in Carnon Crease where furze could be gathered for fires. Most tenants leased 2 or 3 acres, some sublet their land and house, some kept lodgers. Killiganoon and Tregie were large private estates. Most of the rest of the land was owned by Lord Falmouth, Sir Charles Lemon and Lanhydrock estate. These had to keep the land in good order, risk their money in mining, and consider the welfare and employment of their tenants.

Thanks to the present day occupants you can see most of the houses of the tithe map still, some beautifully modernised, some retaining features from 150 years ago. There were on average 5 people to each house, half of them less than 20 years old, the men often employed as miners and labourers, the children also from the age of 12 years. Women and girls were servants, dressmakers and labourers, kept house and small-holding, and managed the family budget, health and education. Roads were rough and narrow in the first half of the 19th century and transport was helped by small Cornish horses and donkeys. As roads were improved on the advice of William McAdam wheels became practical. Tilling the land was by hand tools on small-holdings and by horse power on large farms, until steam machinery was available for hire.

TITHING

The 1842 Tithe map is an assessment of rent charges to be paid instead of one tenth of the produce which was previously owed to the rector for the upkeep of the poor and to the vicar.

A document of 1630 (P64) enumerates exactly what tithes had to be paid in Feock:

"Hee that hath five Kyne to pay all Butter and Cheese of Nyne dayes gatherings the Cheese salted and well seasoned the Butter unsalted, Five Cheeses on the first Sunday after Midsomer the other Fower Cheeses and a Loafe of Butter after Lammas.
Hee that hath seven Calves a Tythinges Calfe Hee that hath seven Lambes a Tythe Lambe For Piggs and Geese in like Sorte
For the milke of everey Ewe to pay a Farthing
For Woll, Horse Coltes, Mare Coltes, Hemp and Flax, Apples, Peares, Plums, Cherries, Eggs, Haye, Leekes, Onions, Garlick one tenth
For everey Fisher Boate that goeth to see a fishinge to pay the tenth Fish, the Viccar to allowe the tenth for Salt and Bayte
For all Barges and Boates that carrey Sande fower pence of the Noble of one halfe of their gaine
Tynners beinge adventurers to paye according to conscience
All Peas and Beanes tylled within the pishe tythed as here to fore."

THE 1842 FEOCK TITHE MAP (inside back cover)
From fief to farm, from manor to messuage, from ploughland to plot
From peas to pence

By 1842 tithes were owned not by a rector but by lay men, in the case of Carnon Downs largely by Thomas Gwatkin of Killiow whose family acquired them from the Gregor family. Edward Boscawen owned tithes of part of Tregie and Thomas Messer Simmons owned tithes of Killiganoon and Halgarnick. The vicar of Feock was entitled to an exact small portion. They no longer collected butter and lambs but a sum of money. Every plot of land was drawn on a map and numbered, over a thousand of them, and a list was made in a book of each plot with its landowner, tenant, sub-tenants, acreage, value, and the sum of money to be paid to the tithe owner. In effect it was a tax on land. The map and list are preserved in Cornwall Record Office. The map is large, 180x266 cm., and a line 26 cm. long represents 30 chains. It is fragile, tattered in parts and repaired; It must not be touched, traced or photocopied. A microfiche copy is offered but is too faint and scratched to be read. The useful map in Feock Parish History book 1 was made I think by copying tenants onto a later O.S. map. Most of the land was owned by the big three estates, Lemon, Boscawen and Agar-Robartes, Killiganoon was owned by Thomas Simmons, and small plots were owned by Hill, Enys and Hugos. Nearly all the land is described as arable, that is it was capable of being tilled, some near streams is 'meadow', and a 37 acre patch between Old Carnon Hill and the top Bissoe Road is 'waste'.

The work was done by short-term tenants who leased a plot or two, and lived on the profits of the land, while subject to strict conditions of good husbandry, that is improving fertility and often having to build or repair a house, and allowing the landlord certain rights, access to water for instance or the right to dig for minerals and convey them.

It happens that a series of censuses at 10-year intervals began in 1841. The Feock ones list in neat handwriting the inhabitants with ages and occupations. Addresses are not given, only the name of a road or farm or just 'Carnon Downs'. They are roughly in geographical order so that Carnon Downs people are distinguishable from the rest of Feock parish. There are 112 households and 600 people listed in the area now called Carnon Downs, that is from Treliever to Come-to-good, and from Chyreen and Killiganoon to bottom Bissoe Road. The detective work is to match surnames found in the census to the tenants on the tithe map. Ideally every tenant with his family could then be placed in his own home on the map. Happily in some cases this is possible, but there are limits. For instance some tenants leased several houses and sublet them, many tenancies were for fields without houses, people moved house often so that between censuses there were changes, and some surnames occur in many households while others are in the census but not in the tithe map list.

The overall picture is that by 1842 most of the land was tenanted and farmed in plots of all sizes. Most of the men and children over 12 years of age had jobs outside their homes, and most of the married women did not. On average there were 6 people to a house, sometimes including lodgers, visitors and servants. Good housekeeping, including fetching water, burying sewage, weeding, manure, carrying furze, milking, preserving meat, were vital.

Landowners were still ultimately responsible for the land, and tenants, having no long-term security, could not be expected to plan for years ahead. In bad times it was the landowners that worried about diseased potatoes, shortage of hay, the price of corn. Not until 1920 did tenants on a large scale buy their own plots and become farmers on scattered settlements in the western end of Feock parish.

In the following pages are the histories of some of these settlements.

TRETHEWEY LANDS
A good place to start

In the triangular traffic island in the middle of the village opposite Tyrrell's is Trethewey Cottage, not yet built in 1842, but the plot was tenanted by William Gerrish, aged 40, mason, who built Devoran Church and chapel. He leased 6 acres on both sides of the main road, and lived in Pine Cottage with his wife Elizabeth and 4 sons and 4 daughters aged 1 to 17. By 1851 he was a master mason employing 5 men, and his sons Edward, William and Stephen were masons also. None of his children were at school. By 1861 3 elder sons had left and Joseph, 21, was a mason and Ellen a scholar. In 1871 only his wife and Ellen were at home.

Why did he call his land Trethewey?

Not only William Gerrish's land but scores of acres from Higher

Devoran in the east to Treliever in the west are recorded as 'Trethewey Lands'. They include Clydia, Chiverton, Carnon Wollas, Ringwell and Dower Ruth. Two families shared Devoran Wartha and its tenements, Elizabeth and Alex Allen, and Alex's cousins the brothers John and Richard Hendra. Richard left in his will in 1734 lands and tinbounds in Kea to his wife Jane for the maintenance of their daughter Blanch; the district around Hugus in Kea is still known as Blanchland. Long before, in 1327, the subsidy rolls listed an Osbert Blanchland in Kea. John in 1716 willed his estate in Carnon Crease for the maintenance of his son John. (WH1385)

Then came the namesake of all this land: Humphrey Betty Trethewey, yeoman, of St Stephen-in-Brannel, married Blanch Hendra, and in 1756 a Thomas Trethewey leased parts of Devoran Wartha, Gwelhedgio and Treliever for a thousand years to William Lemon. Gwelhedgio or Wheal Hediowe was part of Caledgy or Clydia. In 1763 trustees of William Lemon leased a tenement part of Wheal Hediowe to Dan Clift tinner who 'must build a good strong dwelling house at his own cost' and pay 10 guineas. (WH 1390-1404) William Lemon became the landlord at last in 1808 when his steward Paynter paid £1050 for the Trethewey lands.

Each part of this acquisition is a story of its own. The legal writing is foreign to an amateur, but provides an atmosphere of the times. Something like this happened:

Treliever

It was leased in 1815 to William Hancock of Kenwyn who borrowed for the purpose £150 from William Kessell. 7 years later Mary Brewinney of Helston was lending £158 to Jennifer Kessell and £48 to William Hancock. But the lease passed to John Tregoning of Gwennap who began negotiations to sell to George, Charles and Robert Fox and John Williams of Gwennap for £465.

William's lease was determinable (ie finished) on the deaths of William, Jane and Elizabeth Hancock. So John Tregoning paid £63 for it to Jane Hill, widow of Helston, in 1822:
'together with all waste lands of Jane Hill extending westerly so far as to join the lands of Right Honorable Lord de Dunstanville, and to pay 13/4

and tax and £2.2.0 for an heriot immediately after the death and deceases of John Simmons Tregoning and William Henry Tregoning and Richard Williams. The lease is for 99 years 'if those three so long shall live' for which proof must be shown.

'but reserved to Jane Hill all tin lead and copper ores quarries clay marle and liberty of ingress and egress of her servants to dig to land dress and carry and to sink shafts erect houses and engines and machines for draining, and liberty to let commons and to convey and divert water, and all trees with lops and shreds thereof, to carry away bark, and also liberty for her friends to hunt hawk fish and fowl, and tenant shall show to Jane Hill that the three lives still live and keep premises in order and provide one good labourer to assist in cleansing and ridding up all watercourses and passages of water leading to Carnon Mills one day in every year or more often if required.'

Rent of £1.5.8 was to be paid at Christmas, Lady Day, Midsummer, and Michaelmas.

'This indenture made the 25th day of July in the third year of the reign of our sovereign lord George IV by the grace of God ...' (TLP308)

Treliever was then occupied by Ann Watts and then Richard Hendra, until in 1830 Sir Charles Lemon leased an acre of it, with garden and dwelling house, to his gamekeeper John Lobb of Mylor for £61, with all the reservations imposed on John Tregoning.

A more unusual transaction occurred in 1840. For £425 Treliever was bought by The Friendly Society of Carharrack. Trustees, all from Gwennap, were:

George Croker Fox
Robert Were Fox
John Williams of Burncoose
Charles Fox of Perran Wharf
Samuel Michell farmer
Tristram Powning butcher
Dennis Martin butcher

Samuel Polkinghorne miller
William Reed farmer
Grenfell Halse miner.

The last six were the holders of the land. In addition to the reservations of 1822 any land with rails, ie Redruth & Chasewater railway, and near the river was excepted, and the holders must not cut trees, must upkeep the land, must manage and manure according to the rules of good husbandry, must cleanse the leats watercourses and passages for water to Carnon Mill, and must provide evidence of the 3 lives being still alive even if they are in foreign parts.

The tithe map describes Treliever as owned by Harriet, Maria and Jane Hill (not by Sir Charles Lemon), leased to Carharrack tradesmen, and occupied by Samuel Michell with 21 acres, and by William Lobb, with one acre and a house between Treliever and Ringwell Farm and on the same side of Bissoe Lane.

Samuel Michell, 40 in 1841, was a copper miner as well as a farmer. Living with him were his wife, 4 sons of which 2 were 15 and were a copper miner and an agricultural labourer, 3 daughters aged 2 to 10, and an agricultural labourer, Richard Williams aged 25. Bissoe Road through Ringwell and Treliever was then a route from Devoran to Perranwell via Dunstan's Ford, and to Bissoe and Carharrack. There was no road along the Carnon river from Devoran; Instead there was the Redruth & Chasewater railway with horses pulling 60,000 tons of copper ore seawards in a year, and 15,000 tons of Welsh coal up the line, before there were steam locomotives. The Carnon river was a widespread swamp, a heap of mining silt with men and boys and wheelbarrows and temporary roadways. Mr Michell's land, wet as it was below, was on both sides of the railway, and he was farming at a junction of Sir Charles Lemon's and Earl Falmouth's mining land.

In 1863 the viaduct of the railway to Falmouth was built across Treliever land.

Treliever was sold freehold in 1913 to John Tippett of Chacewater.

'All messuages, buildings, barns and stables and all closes and pieces of meadow and pasture, 16 acres, 2 roods and 7 poles, in occupation of George Pascoe, except for the land used by the Cornwall Railway company, including both sides of the viaduct.' The fields were described as 'waste, seven of grass, one with a root crop, and garden'...

Dower Ruth

This steep site below the Falmouth Railway, now derelict and furnished with broken makeshift buildings, farm machinery and cars, appears in the estate papers of Earl Falmouth and Lanhydrock. It is remembered as the home of Miss Rae who lived in a railway carriage and took in stray dogs. Dower Ruth seems to mean 'Red River', and there is a river at the

Carnon Wollas, Carnon Crease, Treliever, Dower Ruth, Ringwell in 1842.
Landowners:

A	Anna Maria Agar
L	Sir Charles Lemon
F	Earl Falmouth
H.W.E.	Hugo Warren and Enys
H.M.J.H..	Harriet, Maria and Jane Hill
A.L.B.	Agar, Lemon and Bunt

Scale   ←————— 700 metres —————→

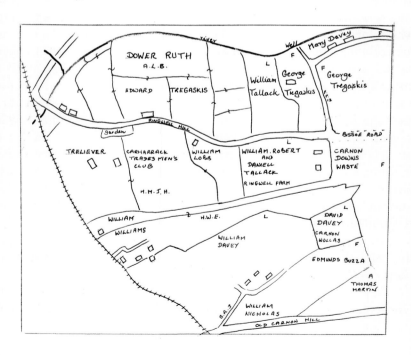

bottom, the same that floods the road at Treliever, not at all red now. On the tithe map it is shown at the bottom of Ringwell Hill opposite Treliever, ten acres with two dwellings on it, owned by Honorable Maria Anna Agar and Sir Charles Lemon and William Bunt and occupied by Edward Tregaskis. All the land is described as meadow which usually means wet grass.

Edward Tregaskis, then 59, was farming Middle Devoran with his wife, sons Edward and Thomas, 20 and 19, daughters 26 and 15, and a servant aged 20. Also at Middle Devoran was George Tregaskis, 30, who held land up the road at what is now 'The Valley' . A Thomas Tregaskis founded the chapel at Hicks Mill.

Dower Ruth was recorded over a century before the tithe map. In 1696 it was a 'parcel of the manor of Tussaven' with house and garden, house and orchard, and some common, and in 1745 it was leased to Thomas Harvey, yeoman, for £21 and rent 6/8 for ten years if Thomas and his children 'so long shall live'. In 1750 the lease was surrendered to John Hendra for 99 years and on three lives, himself, his wife Jane and Alice aged 14 months. (CL/1/129) Edward Tregaskis had to pay a tithe of 12/- to the vicar and 19/- to Gwatkin. Mrs Gummow, living there in 1922, paid less because some land had been taken from her by Great Western Railway to widen the bridge. (WH 1898)

On a precipitous north-facing slope boggy at the bottom it promises ill as farmland; maybe its importance was the water supply and its closeness to mining country.

Ringwell

It is possible that Bissoe Lane, from the centre of Carnon Downs, past Ringwell 'The Valley', Dower Ruth and Treliever to the river crossings at Dunstan's Ford and Bissoe was part of the route from King Harry Passage to Penryn and Helston when Old Carnon Hill was ruinous. Gascoyne in 1699 distinctly drew a road bridge at the bottom of Old Carnon Hill and no road from Tregie to Higher Carnon. Then Martyn in 1748 omits the Old Carnon Hill bridge and draws a crossing at Higher Carnon. In 1784 Ringwell appears for the first time marked as a farm on a road to Higher Carnon where there is a river crossing to Perranwell. The 1842 tithe map shows it as several smallholdings on both sides of the road, the south side owned by Sir Charles Lemon and the north side by Lemon and Earl Falmouth.

There was a road, now F.P. 13, opposite Ringwell Farm, which was the boundary between Lemon and Falmouth land, and George Tregaskis of Middle Devoran occupied 4 acres on both sides of it and let a house and orchard to William Scobell, a copper miner aged 30 in 1841 with a wife and a servant Elizabeth aged 12. The road leads down to the river which flows from Quenchwell and Enenezer, and there lived Mary Davey on 6 acres with house and orchard. She was a widow with a son James, tin miner, and two children aged 11 and 3. The northward spur of F.P. 13, now not traceable, led to a well which is still there on the river bank.

Ringwell Farm on the south side of the road was occupied by William, Robert and Daniell Tallack, perhaps the same people called Retallack who farmed Tregie. There were several other residents at Ringwell Farm in 1841: Amelia, 20, and Jane, 20, dressmaker, Richard Scoble, tin miner, with wife and 4 sons of whom 2 15-year-olds were also tin miners, and a daughter, 12; and Margaret Burroughs with Jane and John, and John Davis, 15, labourer. Here was a crowd of residents surrounded by largely waste land. Bissoe Road from Ringwell to Heath Farm was unfenced and on the south side was Lord Falmouth's trackless waste, on the north side a patch of turbary (where the public had a right to dig peat) and to the south William Williams had 25 acres, some of it waste, some meadow.

More than a century before the tithe map Ringwell Farm was occupied by a Woolcock family. Sir William Lemon let it in 1788 to his grandson William Dingle, tinner, describing it as 'late occupied by Hopson Woolcock' and 'part of Treliever'. The will of a Hopson Woolcock is in the Record Office still (APW 2188), hard to read so imperfectly reproduced below:

'In the name of God amen the twenty-seventh day of July in the year of our Lord God 1732 I Hopson Woolcock of the parish of Feock in the county of Cornwall yeoman being sick and weak in body but of perfect mind thanks be given to God for the same, calling to mind the mortality of my body, knowing it is appointed for all men to die do make and ordain this my last will and testament, principally first and full I give and recommend my soul into the hands of God who gave it and my body to be burned in a Christian manner ... my well beloved wife and as touching such worldly estate as it hath pleased God to bless me with in this life I give devise and dispose in the following manner. I give to my well beloved son Hopson Woolcock my black mare and best saddle and bridle. I give to my well beloved wife whom I constitute make and ordain ffaith Woolcock my only sow (?) ... of this my last will and testament all my goods moveable and immoveable bills bonds and credits together my chattles estates by her freely to be possessed with this proviso if she marry again I give her but £5 ... to be divided alike between my children.

I give to the poor widdows of the parish of Feock 5 shillings to be distributed ...

Signed, sealed in the presence of us

Richard Hendra'

Clydia
Gweeleheggiowe, Calleggy, Gwealhedgio, Caledgy, Calidgy, Gelidgey, Gwelhidgeo, Wheal Hediowe ...

All of these names appear in the Lemon estate files under the title 'Trethewey Lands', and include holdings on both sides of the upper half of Old Carnon Hill, and the east side of the main road as far as the village hall. With Higher Devoran Farm, Clydia was the major part of Sir William Lemon's land in the Feock parish, bordered to the south-east by Agar land and in other directions by Lord Falmouth's. On this land there were no railway, no mining, no smelting, but good manured farmland, orchards and tenant farmers.

Records go back to 1703 when Gweeleheggiowe was leased for £148 to John Hendra, presumably brother of Richard whose daughter Blanch married Humphrey Betty Trethewey. A stiff brown speckled parchment states:

'Hon Lord de Longeville Sir John Talbot Geo Slingsby Esq Francis Arundell Esq Chas Bonython Esq John Cooke gent to John Hendra jun of Feock yeoman Gweeleheggiowe in Feock part of manor of Allet the messuage and tenement with all houses orchards gardens lands meadows pastures and waste to John Hendra and heirs for ever'

There follow seven signatures and red wax seals. (WH 1376)

'Forever' lasted half a century. In 1756 Sir William leased for 1000 years from Humphrey and Thomas Trethewey a moiety of Higher Devoran and Gwellhedgio and Treliever and the next year agreed with Mr Trethewey for purchase of these 'Trethewey Lands" for £800.

Some tenements were let:

In 1763: 'Executors of William Lemon to Dan Clift tinner tenement part of Lower Wheal Hediowe part of Caledgy late occupied by Jas Dennis and after him Michael Harris. Lessee must build a good strong dwelling house at his own cost and pay £10.10.0' (WH 1394)

Note the name Dinnis. What is now called Higher Devoran was then called Dinnis and what is now Middle Devoran was called Higher Devoran. It is not easy to know which is which in old parchments. Dinnis appears on O.S. maps 1813 and 1860 but not on the 1842 tithe map. Before the A39 was built through Devoran in 1830 the Devoran farms were on the same block of land as Clydia. So the house to be built by Dan Clift could be at Higher Devoran.

Other houses under the name of Caledgy, variously spelt, and included in Sir Charles Lemon's Trethewey Lands are:

Lower Clydia, now Old School House, at the bottom of Wellington Place lane, occupied in 1842 by William Daniell, 55, agricultural labourer, with his wife and sons John, 24, Samuel, 20, Thomas, 15, all miners.

Clydia, now on the slip road, house, meadow, vineyard and 2 fields, occupied by William Williams of Higher Devoran.

Higher Clydia, now the trio of houses Penboa, Fentynyow-an-Penty and Sunnyside, then 2 houses, 2 plots and an orchard, occupied by Nathaniel Trengrove (teacher?), and Stephen Gay, 60, coal porter, with his wife and son, 20, also a coal porter.

Halwyn, now on the slip road, occupied by William Williams.

Trerise, and a house immediately below, and the Smithy house now Tyrrells, occupied by Stephen Martin, grocer, 62, with his wife and a girl servant, 16.

Trerise

Chiverton occupied by William Williams

A house at the entrance to Middle Devoran. It was demolished for the building of the bypass.

Agar Farm did not exist until later. The land was farmed by Edward Tregaskis and Stephen Martin.

Pine Cottage, home of William Gerrish, who leased fields on both sides of Forth Coth, north of Staggy Lane on the west side and on the east what is now Carnon Crescent.

Chiverton

Deeds and documents relating to this house and fields along the south side of Smithy Lane, all part of the Trethewey Lands, take us further.

In 1862 Sir Charles Lemon leased to Thomas Dunstan woodman of Kea '4 acres at Carnon Common enclosed by Richard Hobbs on right side of old Truro to Penryn road and occupied by William Williams, on the lives of Thomas, 35, and his wife Jane, 34, for 99 years if they should so long happen to live.'

It seems therefore that this piece of land had been 'common' like Lord Falmouth's 37 acres between Bissoe Road and Old Carnon Hill, and that Richard Hobbs was permitted by Sir Charles to enclose and occupy it for as long as he and his wife remained alive up to 99 years. In this way wild land bit by bit was enclosed and cultivated and often the tenant was obliged to build or to repair a house on it. Tenancies were on three lives, that is terminated when the last of the three named people, usually children, died. This arrangement provided some security for the next generation, but left the original tenant homeless if the three names died young, or even if they emigrated and could not be proved to be alive.

By the time of the next lease in 1873 the Trethewey Lands had been inherited by retired Lieutenant- Colonel Arthur Tremayne, nephew of Sir Charles Lemon. The mid-nineteenth century mining boom was slumping, big landowners had impoverished tenants, and emigration reduced the population. The Corn Laws, designed after 1815 to benefit farmers by limiting the import of cheap corn, were abolished in 1840 to benefit the increasing urban population, and yet the price of corn rose because of poor harvests. Suddenly in 1874 the new railways in America brought corn to Atlantic ports and so to England. Farmers turned 'from corn to horn', that is from arable to cattle, and experienced a slump of their own. It was a time of irreversible changes: the Cornwall Railway, opened in 1859, enabled fish and flowers, potatoes and broccoli to be sent rapidly upcountry, and brought tourists; Bishop Benson arrived to revive the Church of England and work started on Truro Cathedral; school boards were created to provide primary education for all and were empowered to charge ratepayers for it.

Chiverton was leased in 1873 to William Treganown, agent, and in 1895 to John and Elizabeth Dunstan.

Trethewey Lands at the top of Old Carnon Hill
Above Clydia and Higher Clydia in 1842 William Williams, Stephen Martin, Nathaniel Trengrove and William Gerrish all leased Lemon fields. William Williams of Higher Devoran had a meadow, the wet bit below Clydia, a vineyard and a house where is now Halwyn, and the south side of Smithy Lane including Chiverton. Stephen Martin held fields on the north side of Smithy Lane, now Parc-an-Creeg, the cottage which became Webber and Jenning's smithy and later Tyrrell's, and Trerise with its cowshed and loft used as a dame school. Briar Cottage is not on the 1842 map. Its site was part of Higher Devoran farm and separated from Halwyn by the new Falmouth Road in the 1830s; later in the century the house was built and it became a useful overnight stop for passing traffic and holidaymakers.

Pine Tree Cottage
Here lived William Gerrish, famed for having built Devoran church in 1856, houses in Devoran and perhaps its chapel. He held the fields on both sides of the main road from Staggy Lane to its chapel and including Carnon Crescent. He had also the triangle of land between the old and the new Falmouth roads, the only piece of the Trethewey Lands which still bears the name; he had not yet built a house on it in 1842.

Bryher (Briar)

With his large family he had need of living space. He was born in Falmouth in 1801 and by 1841 he was living in Pine Tree Cottage with his wife Elizabeth and four sons and four daughters. Ten years on he was recorded as a Master Mason, the three eldest sons, Edward, 27, William, 25, and Stephen, 18, were all masons and still living with him, and he had another son, Joseph, 10. His daughter Sarah married Nicholas Tallack, waterman of Narabo, and daughter Emily married James Michell, labourer of Carnon Downs. Meanwhile he had two more children, Jeremiah and Ellen. Another daughter appears in the marriage registers, Susan, widow, who married Daniell Retallack of Tregie in 1859; this is a mystery because a daughter called Susan had not previously appeared in the censuses and there was a Sarah, not a Susan, at Tregie.

By 1861 the household was reduced to his wife, Joseph, a mason and Ellen, 16, a scholar. She was the only member of the family who went to school it seems, and in 1871 she married James Davey, skindresser, son of James Davey, a miner. William at 70 described himself as 'owner of houses', retired.

He and his four sons, all masons, must have left examples of their trade in Feock parish and elsewhere, as well as the land on which the centre of Carnon Downs was built in the 1930s. Yet he managed his business without being able to write his name. Alfred Jenkin, agent of Lanhydrock, wrote in 1841: 'about Gerrish's tender to building the cottage at Devoran I send thee his tender and wish him to put a dry pen on the letters of his name as if he were writing it and then will please to put thy name under the word "witness".'

Devoran Wartha
Higher Devoran or Defran or Deveryan Wartha

The earliest surviving document naming Devoran Wartha is dated 1679, in the reign of Charles II, and is a lease and sale for £198 from William Tonn gent to Elizabeth Allen widow, of the property occupied by John and Richard Hendra, and four years later leased by Elizabeth Allen to Richard Hendra. Alex Allen willed the moiety then occupied by his cousin John Hendra to John Allen junior. The word 'moiety' recurs through the

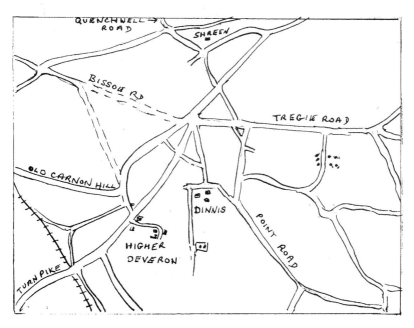

From O.S. 1813 map with railway and new turnpike added.
Present Higher Devoran is called Dinnis and present
Middle Devoran is called Higher Deveron

Higher Devoran
Market Road
B.R.24

next two centuries. In 1730 Richard Hendra and Thomas Pearce agreed to divide the property between them, and Humphrey Betty Trethewey from St. Stephen in Brannel married Blanch Hendra and so possessed the Hendra moiety. A parchment of 1755 about 80 cm. square, decorated with a portrait of George II and relating to Higher Devoran but eroded by mould, has attached to it a tin containing a crumbled seal, a tiny feather and a crinkly ginger hair. (WH 1379)

Exactly what Humphrey had acquired is uncertain because Ordnance Survey maps of 1813 and 1860 show 'Higher Devoran' where now is Middle Devoran and what is now Higher Devoran is labelled 'Dinnis'. The 1842 tithe map shows Higher Devoran as 67 acres on its present day site, with Middle Devoran with 50 acres to the south of it and part of the Lanhydrock estate. Signatures of three Dinnises appear on one document, and an inventory of 1722 records that 'John Dinnis had 35 sheep worth 5/- each, and two cows and a yearling worth about £2 each.' (F.P.H. IV p.7)

It was good farm land on a south-facing slope, with streams to the east and west and sufficiently far from industrial Carnon and Devoran for comfort, yet near enough for tenants to find work there.

There were other lessees in the 18th century, occupying 'a moiety of Devoran Wartha': Edward Pearce surgeon to Phil Watkins and his son Robert; Michael Allen son of John Allen deceased to John Thomas of Truro and William Curgenwen of St. Michael Penkevil.

In 1763 Dan Clift of Feock tinner, was to 'erect within 4 years and build and finish at his own cost a good strong dwelling house' and pay £10. 10. 0 for a 'tenement lately occupied by James Dinnis ... formerly enclosed and built on part of a croft called Lower Wheal Hediowe with meadow part of Caledgey.'   (WH 1394)

Dan Clift is not recorded again. In 1784 Phil Watkins gent leased to John Dunstan yeoman 'the lately erected dwelling house and one acre of land enclosed on Devoran Downs with newly erected smith's shop'.

There is a detailed description of Devoran Wartha at the time when Humphrey Trethewey bought it and agreed with Mr Allen to share its occupation.

Trethewey's share:

The new house. Hall, parlour, cellar and chambers, stairs, ground to build chimney outside the hall, court, linney house. Except Mr Allen has privilege to make cider that grows on the premises when not in use at the cyder press of H.B. Trethewey, repairing half the press and utensils, and foot passage through the court at reasonable hours.

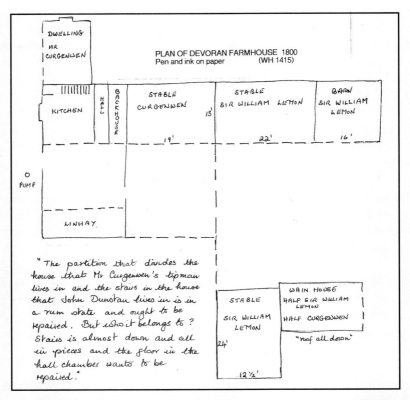

PLAN OF DEVORAN FARMHOUSE 1800
Pen and ink on paper   (WH 1415)

DWELLING
MR
CURGENWEN

KITCHEN | HALL | BACKHOUSE | STABLE CURGENWEN 19' | STABLE SIR WILLIAM LEMON 22' | BARN SIR WILLIAM LEMON 16'

13'

⊙ PUMP

LINHAY

"The partition that divides the house that Mr Curgenwen's tipman lives in and the stairs in the house that John Dunstan lives in is in a rum state and ought to be repaired. But who it belongs to? Stairs is almost down and all in pieces and the floor in the hall chamber wants to be repaired."

STABLE SIR WILLIAM LEMON 24' 12½'

WAIN HOUSE HALF SIR WILLIAM LEMON HALF CURGENWEN   "roof all down"

H.B. Trethewey has higher half of barn with little house adjoining and partition to be made between the bothy and the oxen house with half the wain house, wain house to be repaired by both, and when reed serves to repair the wain house upon refusal to help within 18 days either loses right therein.

H.B.T. to have Park Bower, Lower Meadow, Lower Parc and Lower Parc Coose and usual ways to drive any sort of quick stuff and carry any sort of carriage. H.B.T. to have orchard under Parc Adventon, wain house orchard and mowhay orchard and higher mowhay and former cellar and hopyard and footway to pass. One half of pump or wellyard to make wood fuel and turf therein and the ancient way of carrying wood fuel turf and dressing, and repair one half of pump, and a way for water ... and way through Parc Brose to the tenement of Gweal any sort of quickstuff or carriage ...

(Continues on page 49.)

The tumulus at Parc-an-Creeg
Photos by John Crowe

THIS MOUND OR ROUND BARROW
IS A TOMB OF THE EARLY AND
MIDDLE BRONZE AGE PERIOD
(c.1800–c.800 B.C.)

IT IS PROTECTED UNDER THE ANCIENT MONUMENTS
ACTS (1913–1953) AND IT IS AN OFFENCE
TO INJURE OR DEFACE IT

MINISTRY OF PUBLIC BUILDING AND WORKS

Above:
The Carnon
Viaduct, seen from
the same spot as
Lamorna Birch's
1932 painting,
"Summer Holiday"

Left:
Higher Carnon
Ford

Ringwell Farm

The Croft

Carnon Wollas

Park Farm

Devoran water supply on
bottom Bissoe Road
opposite "Poplars"

Clydia: well and windlass

Claypit field (taken from Surgery)

Meadow Cottage, home of Edward Olive junior

Cloam oven in fireplace at Meadow Cottage

Ashtree Cottage well   (Photo John Crowe)

Heath Farm (Photo John Crowe)

The farm's miniature Shetland ponies

Middle Devoran Farm killing house (Photo John Crowe)

Higher Devoran Farm building (Photo John Crowe)

Footpath 26

Footpath 23 from Point Road to Gateshead (Broadway)

William Pearce's stable on footpath 23

Pine Tree Cottage

Trethewey (Photo John Crowe)

Gateshead (now Broadway) Cottage (Photo John Crowe)

Trerise

Trerise washhouse

Trerise well

Old Cottage

Aylesford

Victoria's Cottage

Smithy Cottage (Photo John Crowe)

Park View Farm, with mangle

H.B.T. has from corner of linney to corner of cowhouse, all ground within next wainhause orchard to lower end of barn, mowhay, orchard as high up as the old upping stock place and from entry of wain house along to the Downs.

Allen's share:

The old house with chambers, brewhouse, kitchen and house that was called James's then a stable, and lower half of barn and lower mowhay and hay mowhay, bee garden and garden before his door and half well or pumpyard, and to make and lodge wood and turf and repair half the well, Parc Brose, Higher Park, Pound Close, Higher and Lower Meadow, orchards under it. Townplace from linney corner to oxen house corner adjoining lower barn. John Allen not to lodge dung within 5 feet of his barn and stable wall and James's house, and he must keep clear road into court. Higher part of upping stock place. Must keep Downs gate in good repair.

Free passage through townplace and a sanding way. Great Croft from Devoran Lane end to the middle of a burrow to a thorn tree. Croft Rowling.

Trethewey and Allen are to share rates and taxes, to thatch their houses in one another's right, to carry away old thatch, to winnow corn in one another's ground. (WH 1401-1403)

There is a plan of Devoran farmhouse in about 1800 when it was 'in a rum state' and divided between Sir William Lemon and Mr Curgenwen who was later the Lemon agent. (WH 1415)

Sir William Lemon in 1808 for £1080 bought the Trethewey Lands including Devoran Wartha's 22 acres and 10 acres of common and right of common on Carnon Downs. The farm was leased at once to William Williams who still held it in 1842. As a tenant Williams was bound to preserve the fertility of the land.

'the messuage farm and tenement late occupied by John Dunstan and now by William Williams and also that other messuage and farm formerly the lands of William Curgenven lately occupied by John Gay ... reserving to Sir William Lemon all tin lead copper and all mines metals and minerals and stone clay and marle found digged or wrought and liberty to dig for same and erect engines and also liberty to grant lease any part of the commons to persons who may enclose and erect buildings and also reserving all timber with liberty to fell same and also all streams and liberty to divert. Yearly rent to be paid on Lady Day Midsummer Michaelmas and Christmas and William Williams must pay all land taxes and other rates taxes and tithes ... and take all such parish apprentices as shall be imposed and shall execute office of reeve for Manor of Trethewey and do all repairs and on every acre to be tilled shall bring in 10 cartloads of good salt sea sand and mix same with dung and earth according to the rules of good husbandry and after such dressing shall take only 2 crops of grain of which only one is wheat and then leave fallow 3 years at least and shall use on the premises all dung straw compost soil manure and ashes as shall arise at the end of the term (14 years) shall leave same for the use of Sir William Lemon and William Williams shall at his own expense sow and harrow in 6 pounds weight of clover and 12 gallons of ever seed in every acre and not cut any part to hay 2 years successively and after cutting shall bring in 20 cartloads of good dung on every acre and he shall not cut wood from hedges without newmaking casting plashing and doubledyking at the proper time of year while the fields are tilled with wheat. He shall not top or lop any tree, shall not commit any waste. If rent is not paid, Sir William shall be permitted to reenter premises and repossess.

And William Williams shall quietly and peaceably have hold use occupy possess and enjoy the demised premises without hindrance by Sir William Lemon.' (WH1404)

This document is written on torn brown paper and signed by William Williams in black ink. (WH 1415)

William Williams

William Williams was still the tenant of Higher Devoran in 1842, then aged 75 and living with his wife, 15-year-old son and male and female servants called Penna and Woolcock. The census lists his family under Middle Devoran, together with about a dozen other families:

Thomas Martin, 50, with wife and baby
Stephen Carveth, 20, waggon driver
Edward Tregaskis, 59, farmer with wife and 4 children
Phillip Michell, 20,servant
George Tregaskis, 30, with wife, 2 sons and baby
Catherine Trewick, 65, and Catherine Rossiter, 15, both grocers
Richard Coad, 66, farmer and wife
Elizabeth Scoble, 25, Harriet Edes, 15, Thomas Manuell, 15,
    all servants

Middle Devoran was owned by Hon. Anna Maria Agar of Lanhydrock and the principal tenant was Edward Tregaskis who presumably sublet buildings and fields.

During the 1830s the Truro Turnpike Trust made a new road through Carnon Downs to Devoran, now called Forth Coth or Old Road. The older turnpike was Old Carnon Hill. The newer one cut through William Williams' fields, so separating Higher and Middle Clydia on its way to Devoran Bridge, and providing him with an entrance on the main road as an alternative to 'Market Lane', now B.R. 24. More importantly the public could walk from Carnon Downs to Devoran on the new main road instead of through Higher Devoran Farm and Narabo.

But the days of peacefully walking along main roads were beginning to close. Roads were about to be improved. Two more men called William, father and son Macadam, were engaged as surveyors to the Turnpike Trust and undertook to provide more durable roads at no extra cost. Their recommendation was to compact an eight-inch layer of stones of size 2 - 2½ inches and on top of this a two-inch layer of smaller stones. So successful were they that instead of loading mules and horses with harvested crops, hay and manure, farmers could hitch horses to loaded carts. Letters from London, instead of being delivered to packet boats in Falmouth by boys on galloping horses, could be carried in larger quantities by mail coaches.

The fields of Higher Devoran, 67 acres in 1842, all have names: Meadow, Near-the-house Field, Clodgy, Long Clodgy, Great Field, Park Braws, Lower Nonesuch, Great Nonesuch, Four Acres, Great and Lower Clodgy. If Clodgy means lazar house then maybe there was a home for disfigured outcasts in the field immediately above Middle Devoran Lane entrance, bulldozed together with Oak Tree Cottage when the bypass was excavated. (*Journal of Royal Institution of Cornwall* 1965)

A little field tucked into an angle on the north side of the lane was 'Daniell's Meadow'. He was another William, a coal and ore porter, who by 1851 with his wife Anna had six children, the youngest aged six months.

Puzzlingly in 1851 the census records occupants of Higher Devoran, Middle Devoran, Little Devoran, and Devoran Farm where we find Tabitha, 76, widow of William Williams and farmer of 50 acres assisted by her sister, 75, and two more Williams aged 20 and 26, a waggoner and an agricultural labourer, and Jane, 22, a servant. At Higher Devoran meanwhile were William Daniell and three other families and a lone six-year-old William Ball.

By 1861 Tabitha had moved out to live in Carnon Downs with Nicholas Ball, a labourer on the railway, and Devoran Farm's 50 acres were held by Thomas Williams and his son. Ten years later three families were resident at Higher Devoran: John Soloman and his son, agricultural labourers, his wife and his daughter, a dressmaker; Thomas Daniell, a porter on the quay, with wife and 4 children; and Nicholas Tallack, a butcher, with wife and two children. John Langdon remembers that a Captain Sam Williams rented the farm fifty years later.

Carnon Valley

Along the bottom Bissoe Road, on the north side of the line of the Redruth-Chasewater railway from Treliever to the bottom of Old Carnon Hill, there were in 1842 properties in various ownerships, including those of Sir Charles Lemon who was troubled by tenants who dug in the mud of the Carnon river and without permission built roads and bridges and fences. As farmland the slopes had the advantage of facing the afternoon sun,

The Carnon Valley

OLD WOODEN VIADUCT THAT IS TO GO

and there were streams and springs, but there were acres of common amongst the fields which were easily invaded by gorse.

South-east of Treliever there was a strip of Lemon land farmed by William Williams, perhaps the farmer of Higher Devoran, or perhaps the younger Williams at Tresithick who had a wife and 6 children aged 12 to 3. He held also the neighbouring 25 acres of Hugo Warren and Enys land. Today almost under the railway viaduct built in 1863 is Hope Springs, previously called Catervilla or Keatrevilla, glorious with fruit blossom in the spring, home in 1841 to Joseph Jennings, 25, arsenic miner, with wife and 4 children. Next, to the south-east is F.P.5 leading to Oak Farm and Ringwell, and beyond that there are now 2 houses, one at the top and one at the bottom of a quarry, and known as Carnon Crease. The bottom one is on the tithe map, having today a statuesque garden backed by woods and vertical quarry wall. Williams' fields were described as plots, arable, meadow which seems to mean wetland, and waste.

Further south-east on Lemon land there were several houses some of which have totally disappeared. At the bottom of Old Carnon Hill is now B.R.3, a wet sunken lane, boggy at the bottom, hewn through slate through which water drips over mosses and liverworts. At the top is a stony depression into which a bucket could be dipped, and yet the nearest house, Carnon Wollas, is a rough, steep uphill 200 metres away. The tithe map shows 2 houses at the bottom, 2 half-way up and 2 more near Carnon Wollas. One was the home of William Davey, 25, with his wife and 3-month-old daughter, and his farm was 7 plots, 2 crofts, a field, waste and an orchard. Next-door on Falmouth land Edmund Buzza, 40, tin miner with his wife, 5 sons 2 of whom were miners aged 17 and 15 and one was a year old, and 2 daughters, also had an orchard and 7 fields, 3 plots, 2 crofts and a brake. Imagine the wives and children keeping house while the men were away in the mine.

Carnon Wollas is distinctive on the tithe map because it is a square divided into 6 rectangles, and today because it is bounded by parish paths 2, 3, and 4. It is called Wollas (lower) I suppose because it is nearer the sea than Higher Carnon. In 1842 its 6 plots and a house were leased by Sir Charles Lemon to David Davey, 45, arsenic miner, with wife, son and 6 daughters aged 15 to one year.

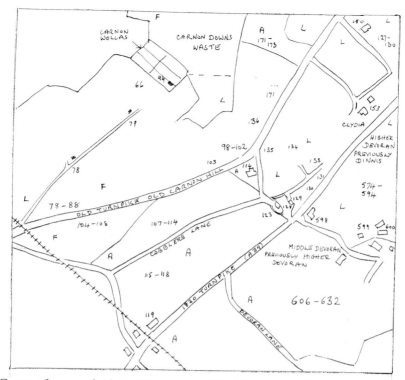

Copy of part of 1842 tithe map with tithe map reference numbers

It is puzzling that parish paths 2, 3, 4, 5 and 6 lead to Carnon Wollas from all directions, making it a hub of pedestrian and horseback travel. A possible reason is that to the south of David Davey were 4 acres of turbary, meaning a public right to dig peat, cut furze and graze animals. There was also on his east border the waste belonging to Lord Falmouth and Sir Charles Lemon to which the public had access until it was enclosed and cultivated in the 20th century. Carnon Wollas was a square island in the midst of wild heath.

Here is a domestic detail:

1783 -1818 'We the undersigned agree to repair the dwelling house at Carnon Crease as proposed by Mr Williams and Mr Manuell'

The spelling is as written in the agreement. 'To take down the frunt corners of the foundation and build them up agean and build up one back corner from the stenwork to the roof and plaster the same inside and repear what plastering is needful and to provide and fix 2 pear of prospals to support the roof and mak a new window and glass it the window to be 2'6" square to make a dreen around the higher part of the house to provide lime stone timber brick glass neals labour carrige of all mateareals.' £5.10.0   Joseph and David Martin. C.M. Hugo would pay. (EN 1313)

Supervision of the industrial activities in the Carnon Valley was a continuing worry to the landowners. Alfred Jenkin, agent to Lanhydrock, wrote in 1859, 'John Vivien must not be allowed to proceed in his filtering and precipitating works until he has signed for a sett.' 'It will not do to allow carts and waggons to be driven over the railways at the quay yet there should be access to it by a good road.'

In the mining slump of the 1880s Captain Arthur Tremayne, inheritor of Lemon estates, was still anxious about his tenants taking liberties in the mud. His agent Smale wrote to his solicitor Whitford, enclosing a hand-drawn map of the Redruth and Chasewater railway track west of Old Carnon Hill, the vitriol works, and opposite the lower fields of Carnon Wollas a bridge coloured in red. His concern was that 'horses and carts are in the habit of going up and down Carnon Creek. Mr Michell, tenant of Carnon Crease, not satisfied with that, has erected a bridge, raised a road and fenced it with iron wire.' Smale was told that Mr Olive raised the road with permission of Mr Anderson. Mr Anderson said he did not permit the road but Mr Whitford did. Landowners' agents and lawyers had to settle such disputes and keep the value of the land, while providing employment and housing. (WH 1409)

FOR SALE FREEHOLD
THE LEMON LANDS IN CARNON DOWNS

The 'Great Mr William Lemon' (1696-1760), from Germoe, worked in copper mines, became manager of Chyandour tin-smelting house, profitably invested his wife's money in Wheal Fortune, Ludgvan, employed John Williams of Scorrier to manage the Poldice mines, and studied as an adult under the master of Truro Grammar School. By luck, hard work and judgement he earned a fortune and bought Carclew. His grandson was Sir William Lemon (1748 -1824) who bought the Trethewey Lands. His elder son William shot himself, leaving a younger son Sir Charles (1784-1868) to inherit. His successor was his nephew, Lieutenant-Colonel Arthur Tremayne, a survivor of the charge of the Light Brigade. A marriage settlement in 1890 gave title of the estate to Captain W.F. Tremayne.

After the first world war changes could not be avoided. Farm land had been neglected while young men were away fighting. Many never returned, many came back crippled, some who survived looked for jobs better paid than labouring in the fields. In June 1920 Captain Tremayne offered his property in Carnon Downs and Kea for sale, freehold. Until then houses and land had been sold on long leases with strict conditions imposed on tenants, the big landlords being ultimately responsible for it and passing it to their descendants in good condition. With the sales tenants became small-holders.

Captain Tremayne was not alone. In September of the same year Lord Falmouth offered his land for sale and in the next year Lady Margaret Boscawen advertised the sale of Tregie. A few sale brochures still exist, brown stained and brittle, and are a valuable account, with maps, of the lots.

SALE OF CARCLEW ESTATE
of
CAPTAIN W.F.TREMAYNE

'The land is well adapted for mixed and dairy farming and small-holdings in a thriving agricultural district' said the brochure. There were reservations:

'All mines minerals ochre granite elvan and stone reserved to person entitled to dig for same and get by on surface or underground without any obligation to leave any support for surface or buildings, with or without horses carts wagons machinery, reasonable compensation to be paid for damage, and to sink pits make roads railways and tramways, deposit store and make merchantible all minerals.

'All leats waters and watercourses and beds banks and sources thereof reserved to person entitled to use and direct same and power to him to pass ... for repairing and cleaning such watercourses. Purchaser may make use of leats ... for farming and domestic purposes but not for irrigation and keep repaired and protected from cattle and not interfere with flow or pollute.

'The purchaser pays tithe, rentcharge and land tax.

'Timber included in sale.'

It is worth reading the schedule of the properties for sale in 1920. There were no main services but the tithe commutation and the land tax had to be paid. The existing tenants, the rent they pay and the length of their tenure are stated, and the outbuildings are listed in more detail than is the house.

Here is a list of the Lemon properties, offered by Captain W.F. Tremayne, numbered as on the sale map.

132 Higher Devoran Farm. 66 acres 3 roods 14 perches let to Richard Williams for 14 years terminating in 1920 for £83 p.a.
    The house contains porch, sitting room, dining room, passage, kitchen, back kitchen, dairy, 5 bedrooms, coal house, fowl house, shed.
    The buildings comprise cart shed, trap house, root house, cow house for 10, implement shed, chaff house, bullock house for 10, root house and barn over, piggery with 6 sties and furnace house, root house, yearling house, three-stall stable and loft over, calves' house.
    The fields are listed with their acreage, most described as arable. The farm was bought by Mr J. Langdon of Middle Devoran.

133 Small-holding 1 acre let to John Teague on yearly tenancy rent £5.
    The house contains 2 sitting rooms, kitchen, back kitchen, 2 bedrooms, box room, wash house and fowl house. Buildings comprise

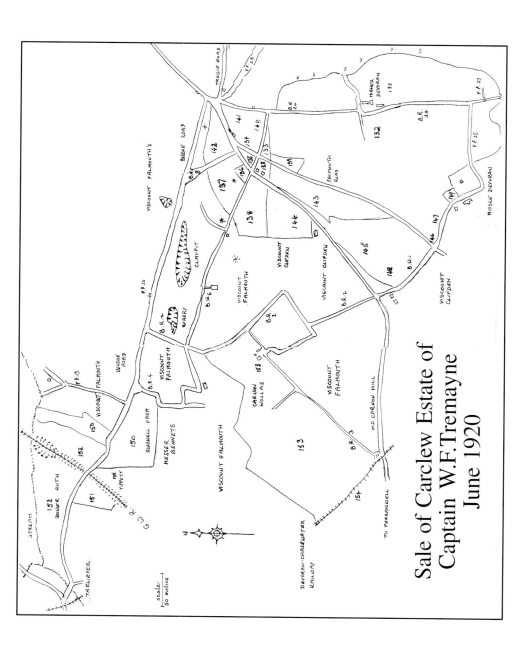

Sale of Carclew Estate of
Captain W.F.Tremayne
June 1920

cowhouse for 5 with loft over, closet and wood house.

This was Trerise, recognisably a farm until 2004 with doves and a sunken bowl with ducks. Mrs Pengilly and Miss Julian are still remembered herding their cows along Smithy Lane. Tom Trebilcock recalled a dame school in the loft. The well and windlass and the fireplace in the wash room are still there.

134 Cottage in 1 acre let to Richard Williams terminating in 1920 rent £20 p.a. Sublet to Mrs Nichols, contains kitchen, sitting room, back kitchen, pantry and 2 bedrooms. Buildings comprise fowl house, stable, trap house and large workshop.

It was in 1842 the home of William Gerrish, mason. Pine Cottage now, it juts on to Forth Coth east side opposite Trethewey. It is said to have been one of many beerhouses in the 19th century.

135 Trethewey house and garden, 34 perches, occupied by Mrs Martin, rack rent £18 p.a. and subject to a lease determinable on death of one life now aged 75.

The house contains porch, sitting room, dining room, kitchen, back kitchen, 3 bedrooms and box room with rain water tank, wash house, closet and good garden.

In 1842 Mr Gerrish owned the triangle of land between Main Road and Old Carnon Hill but there was no house on it.

136 Cottage and garden, 1 rood, let to John Teague, rent £2.1.8, sublet to Mr Webber who bought it and land between Staggy and Smithy Lanes for £175.

Contains sitting room, kitchen, back kitchen, 2 bedrooms, coal house and closet. Webber and Jennings built their Smithy there, and it is now Tyrrell's shop.

137 5 enclosures of land let to John Teague, yearly tenancy £2.

138 Small-holding, 4 acres, occupied by Mr Stephens and subject to a lease determinable on the death of one life now aged 78 years, rent 10 shillings p.a.

The house contains sitting room, kitchen, back kitchen, 3 bedrooms and box room.

Buildings comprise cowhouse for 3 and a pony stable with loft over, tool house and 2 pigs' houses.

This is Chiverton with fields on the south side of Smithy Lane.

139 Poplar House, buildings and land, 3 roods and 15 perches, occupied by J Collins, rack rent £20 p.a. and subject to a lease determinable on death of two lives now aged 76 and 74, rent 5/- p.a.

House contains sitting room, drawing room, dining room, kitchen, pantry and five bedrooms.

Buildings comprise trap house, stable, wash house and loft over.

The house was not there in 1842. It became Briar or Bryher Cottage, now on the slip road from Devoran. It is remembered as a guest house and a welcome stop for tea.

140 Field 1 acre occupied by William Nicholls rack rent £4 p.a.

141 Field 2 acres let to Richard Williams terminating in 1920, rent £2.10.0 p.a.

142 Field 3 acres let to Richard Williams terminating in 1920, rent £4.11.0 p.a.

140-142 are both sides of Forth Coth between Staggy Lane and Village Hall, building sites in 1930s.

143 Smallholding 7 acres, let to W.J. Collins terminating in 1932, rent £19.5.0 p.a.

Two cottages occupied by Mr Dunstan and Miss Nettle each containing sitting room, kitchen, two bedrooms, closet and woodhouse.

Buildings comprise pigs' house, cowhouse for 6 with barn over and large rain water tank, fowl house.

The fields were between Old Carnon Hill and the slip road, the cottages perhaps Halwyn.

144 Three cottages and 5 acres, rack rent £32 p.a. Subject to lease determinable on death of one life now aged 65, rent 6/- p.a.

The cottage occupied by Mrs Davey contains sitting room, kitchen, 2 bedrooms, with wash house, coal house, closet and garden.

The cottage occupied by Miss Davey contains sitting room dining room kitchen and 3 bedrooms with wash house, coal house and closet adjoining.

The cottage occupied by Mr Nicholls contains sitting room, kitchen, wash house and 2 bedrooms.

The land is part arable, part pasture.

The cottages are now called Penboa, Fentynynow an Penty and Sunnyside on Old Carnon Hill. The fields were on the opposite side of the road above Agar Farm.

145 Smallholding 'Clydia', 4 acres now in occupation of J.H. Williams and Mr Woolcock, rent £27.

The house contains sitting room, dining room, kitchen, back kitchen, 3 bedrooms, box room and workshop adjoining.

Land is mostly pasture.

Sold to Mr Woolcock

145a Pasture 1 acre, let to William Collins until 1932, rent £3 p.a.

Rights of entry for collecting water and for the purpose of making and maintaining any works in connection therewith, together with easements for pipes for collecting and conveying water to Devoran reservoir are reserved on payment of rent £1.5.0 p.a. and maintenance of a water trough. This was a strip of land opposite Clydia on main road.

146 Cottage, gardens, buildings and orchard, 1 rood, let to late Mr Jonathan Penrose, rent £8 p.a. The cottage contains sitting room dining room kitchen and 3 bedrooms with closet, tool house and garden adjoining. Fowls' house and large store.

This was Oak Tree Cottage on the north side of the entrance to Middle Devoran. It was razed in 1990 and its site is under the tarmac of the bypass.

147 Field 1 acre, let to Richard Williams terminating in 1920, rent £3 p.a.

148 Smallholding 3 acres in occupation of Mrs Kemp, rack rent £25 p.a. Subject to lease determinable on death of 3 lives now aged 78, 70 and 66, rent £9.10.0 p.a.

The house contains sitting room , dining room, kitchen, back kitchen, 4 bedrooms and box room. The buildings comprise wash house, implement house, pigs' house, coal house, cow house for 5 and two-stall stable.

This must be the 'Old Schoolhouse' in the branch of F.P. 1 which led to Middle Devoran before the main road was built in about 1830. There was once a slaughter house just below it.

149 Field and tennis court, 1 rood 39 perches, in occupation of Mrs Kemp, rack rent £2 p.a., subject to lease determinable on death of 3 lives aged 78, 70 and 66, rent 10/- p.a.

It was immediately north of Middle Devoran farm buildings, the field called Daniell's Meadow in the tithe map.

150 Ringwell Farm 5 acres let to Amos Burrows rent £13 p.a.

House contains sitting room, kitchen, dairy, 2 bedrooms, large rain water tank, wash house, cow house for 3, cow house for 4 and barn over, cart shed.

Pasture, arable, waste and grass, includes a field on north side of Ringwell Hill. Messer Bennett and Mr Tippett own land on west side and Lord Falmouth on east.

Bought by Mr Woolcock

151 One acre let to late Amos Burrows, rent £2 p.a.

152 Dower Ruth 10 acres let to Mrs Gummow, rent £11 p.a., withy plot, arable and pasture.

153 Carnon Wollas 25 acres, occupied by Mr Horton, rack rent £50, lease determinable on death of one life aged 64 rent 16/-. House occupied by Mr Rowe.

House contains kitchen, back kitchen, pantry, wash house, 2 bedrooms, box room.

Cowhouse for 10, cart shed, meal house, two-stall stable and barn over, implement shed, pigs' house, poultry house.

154 One acre, rack rent £22, lease terminable on death of two lives aged 70 and 63, rent 5/- p.a.

Cottage occupied by Mr Courtis contains sitting room, kitchen, 2 bedrooms. Cottage occupied by Mr Francis contains sitting room, kitchen, back kitchen, 3 bedrooms.

Cottage occupied by Mrs Jennings contains sitting room, kitchen, 2 bedrooms

Each with wash house, pigs' house, closet and land.

These houses are on an island of Redruth & Chasewater Railway land between railway and Carnon River.

BOSCAWEN LANDS

While Captain Tremayne could see most of his Trethewey lands across the Carnon river from his house at Carclew, Lord Falmouth was separated from his land in Carnon Downs by the Truro river and some hills in Kea. Tregothnan was built in 1818 for the first Earl Falmouth who was also the fourth viscount of that name. The first viscount, Hugh Boscawen, was visited by his cousin, Celia Fiennes, in 1698, as she rode to and through Cornwall on horseback, and she left a description of his comfortable house on Roseland and the view of distant mines. The third son of a viscount Falmouth, Edward Boscawen, 1711-1761, is famous as 'Old Dreadnought', victor at Puerto Bello, valiant at Carthagena, commander of an East India expedition, Admiral of the Blue.

Earl Falmouth in 1842 owned most of the land north of Bissoe Road as far as the stream, the land on the south side down to the Redruth and Chasewater Railway, fields from Narabo to Chycoose, land on both sides of Point Road and parts of Tresithick. North of Bissoe Road was let in plots of 3 or 4 acres enclosed by hedges and farmed by tenants. The field now next to the surgery and southwards was 37 acres of waste, overgrown, uncultivated, and named 'Carnon Downs'.

Here are some of the tenancies:

George Tregaskis, aged 30, father of three and farming at Middle Devoran, held what is now Ringwell camp or 'The Valley'.

Between the bottom of Old Carnon Hill and F.P.3 was Edmunds Buzza, then 40 and a tin miner, with a wife and 7 children, two of whom, aged 17 and 15, were also tin miners. The only trace of habitation remaining is the well at the top of the footpath.

There were two houses in the fields which became Knights Meadow. Edward Jose, an agricultural labourer with three children, lived on the site of number 22. Number 31 was the home of Edward Olive junior; he was, like his father, a shoemaker, 29 and married, and he tilled the field to the west of him up to the edge of Lord Falmouth's waste. The approach to his house was through F.P. 7 from Bissoe Road, and the house still has its cloam oven.

Edward Olive senior had the house Ashtree in Staggy Lane, as well as the row of cottages now called Trevince, and a house and barns at Ebenezer. He was the founder of the chapel, having started a Sunday school in a barn for 200 children. In 1842 he was 54, married to Honor née James, and with children Samuel, 8, and Elizabeth, Mary, Phillippa and Hannah aged 15 to 3. He came from Gerrans and was a farmer as well as a shoemaker. Twenty years later he was a rate collector and relieving officer of the poor for the parish vestry, with two daughters still at home, and a lodger, William Bassett also a shoemaker, from St. Enoder.

There may have been other daughters, since Tom Trebilcock records that Olive's child Nancy married William Dunstan of Hazeldene. An Elizabeth Olive married John Nicholl of Devoran in 1842. In 1871 'Captain Olive' was still collecting the poor rate, and still a local preacher, and his wife had died.

There were no other houses in Staggy Lane in 1842, and no 'Old Cottage'. The south side of Bissoe Road, Staggy Lane to the main road was leased to the trustees of the chapel in 1925, and they not only built the chapel but let some land on either side of it. Charles Manuell, a porter with 4 children, one a miner, occupied Aylesford in an acre. This house was later the home of Jo Davey. William Murton, a carpenter with 3 children, occupied one rood and built the house 'Victoria'.

The chapel then was the beginning of a village centre on the turnpike with 3 other roads, Bissoe, Quenchwell and Tregie, converging upon it from the wild west and the gentler east.

I shall trace Lord Falmouth's properties from Ringwell up to the main road.

Ringwell camp site, 'The Valley', was sheltered and had the river for water supply. Mary Davey, 55, a widow, had a house, orchard, meadow, moor, plot and croft near the river, wet and on a north-facing slope. Also on the camp site were William Scoble, 30, copper miner, and Richard Scoble, 45, tin miner with a wife and 5 children, and George Tregaskis from Middle Devoran.

William Retallack of Ringwell Farm held plots and crofts further up Ringwell Hill, and above him were Ann and John Michell, part of whose land was turbary.

At the top of the hill and right opposite Lord Falmouth's unfenced waste was what is now Heath Farm. Here Elizabeth Honeychurch held 3 acres, 3 plots and a house. There was one other Honeychurch in Carnon Downs in 1841, a mason aged 55. F.P.12 along the side of Heath Farm crosses F.P.13 and leads to a spring where Thomas Michell, labourer with 7 children from Chyreen, had a house of which no trace remains among the brambles.

Edward Olive held fields from Heath Farm to Trevince, including a house at the entrance to Heath Farm. At Ebenezer he had 2 houses and 2 plots, and in a barn there he started his Sunday school. Trevince was his, described as three plots and a house, and beside it is F.P.9 leading to Charles Dunstan's 8 acres at Trevilla and to the well at Samaria where nearby tenants had the right to draw water at the house of William West, 45, a porter with 2 children. Opposite Treliever in the bend of the lane to Ebenezer was another Edward Olive house.

From Trevince to the main road the only house on the north side of Bissoe Road was Hazeldene opposite Staggy Lane. Here lived William Dunstan and Nancy and 4 children. William was a builder and carpenter and a local preacher into his eighties. His son William became a wheelwright, his daughter Emily a grocer, and Ellen a teacher. Ralph, his youngest, born in 1857,was a pupil teacher at 13, learnt music from the chapel orchestra of flutes and euphonium, learnt there to play piccolo, flute, euphonium, bassoon, clarinet and violin. He composed pieces for a band and played Mozart's Mass on a harmonium. He became a scholar and music master at Westminster College and Southlands, Wesleyan training colleges for teachers. He advised on the installation of the organ at Carnon Downs chapel and is known for his collections of Cornish songs.

Hazeldene

East of Hazeldene one big field let to William Woon, 42, labourer, stretched from Bissoe Road to Valley Lane. Most of it became Manse Road and Forth Noweth in the 1960s and later Parc an Gwarry. William Crowle, blacksmith, had a little strip opposite the chapel and Murton in his tiny plot at Victoria Cottage held also fields opposite. There were two houses on the south side of Valley Lane; John Tregidger, 35, grocer and father of 4, had one, William Woon the other. William West of Samaria held the field opposite his house.

'The Beeches' was let to Elizabeth Burrows who held also a field bordering the lane to Chyreen and a building in a layby in B.R.15. She was 46 and a widow, mother of 9 children, 4 of whom were miners. Next to her on the site of the garden centre were the 7 acres of moor, waste, plots and house of Mary West. This must be where Miss Philbrick and Miss Bowring grew vegetables and flowers for sale from 1939, and which is described in Feock Parish History part IV. From there to Quenchwell chapel fields were let to William Woolcock and to Juliana Dunstan who lived in Satya and its neighbour and in Quenchwell Farm.

Shreen

Chyreen, Chirwyn

The name 'Shreen' seems to cover the present day holdings of Chyreen and Chirwyn, bounded by Kea parish boundary to the north and by B.R.15 to the south-west and B.R.14 sometimes called Ralph's or Rufus lane to the south-east. Both used to be approached mainly from the main Truro - Falmouth road.

The house at Chyreen was occupied in 1842 by Thomas Pengelley, 61, lead smelter, with his wife and 5 children, one of them employed as a carrier. But somewhere were also housed Thomas Michell, 50, labourer, with wife and 7 children, and James Pengelley, 31, shoemaker with wife and 3 children. Nicholas Dunstan occupied Chirwyn, and George Martyn had 5 acres between B.R.15 and F.P.16 and a house on F.P.11.

Thomas Pengelley was still there ten years later, then a coke burner, with his daughter Jane a dressmaker. James Pengelley was then a porter and had 3 more children. In addition Nathaniel Trengrove, 47, had arrived with his wife and 9 children, the eldest at 17 being an agricultural labourer, and the youngest 5 months old.

By 1861 there were no children living there. Nicholas Pengelley, 18, was a lodger and farm labourer, William Trengrove, 25, was a tin miner, William Gluies, 39 was another farm labourer, and Samuel Drake, 60, was a Chelsea Pensioner with his wife 15 years older than himself.

In 1871 all 4 residents had not wives but 'housekeepers', presumably just a matter of language. William Gluies had 3 children, James Nicholls had 3 babies, and two 70-year-olds had moved in: Charles Wasley calling himself 'traveller, tramp', and William Woon from Valley Lane.

Wasleys and Pengelleys

Charles Wasley with his wife Honor were living in Carnon Downs at the time of the first census in 1841, and already they had four sons, of which the eldest, 15, was a miner, and two daughters. He himself was then a

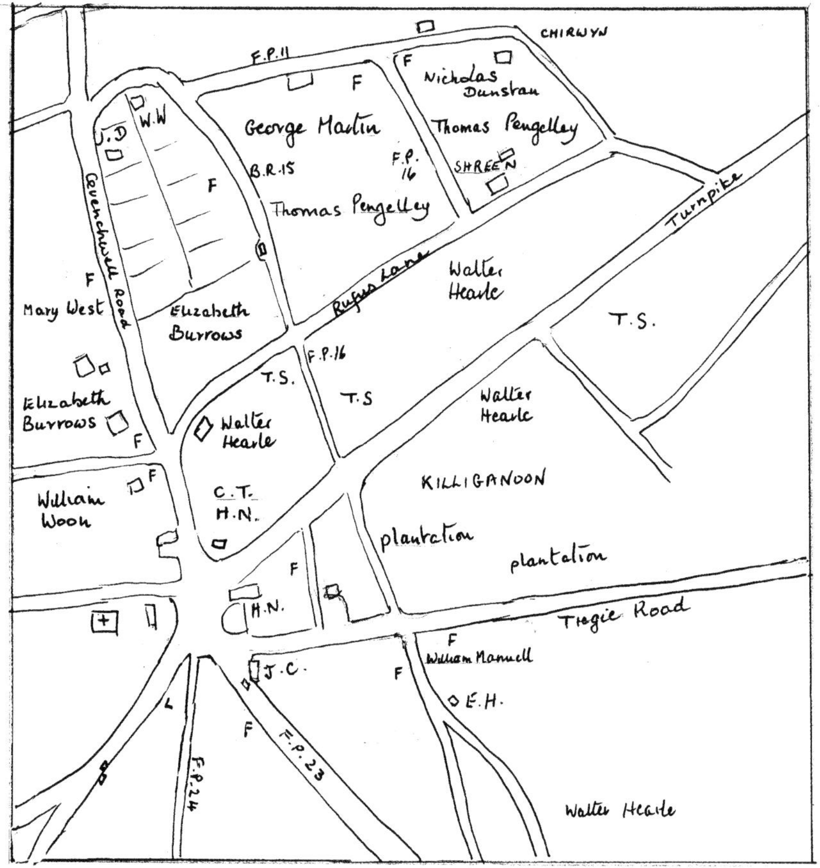

Tenants around SHREEN in 1842

Landlords

F   Lord Falmouth
L   Sir Charles Lemon
T.S.   Thomas Simmons
E.H.   Elizabeth Hugo

Tenants

J.D.   Juliana Dunstan
W.W.   William Woolcock
C.T.   Charles Trengrove
H.N.   Henry Nicholls
J.C.   James Collins

pilot and in the next census a 'waterman'. Two of his sons, Fred and James, aged 8 and 2 in 1841, were replaced in 1851 by Fred and James aged 4 and 2. Maybe two boys died and two more were born. His son William became a porter and married Susan Monk of Mylor.

Inside the chapel on the north-facing wall is a memorial: 'window installed in honoured memory of William James Pengelley who was formerly a scholar, worshipper and chorister in this church, born at Carnon Downs 19.9.1890, died in Canada 19.10.1928.'

Who was he? William Wasley and Susan Monk had a daughter Bessie who married a James Henry Pengelley and had eleven children. William James was the eldest of those.

Honor, the wife and housekeeper of Charles Wasley is remembered in a story told by Tom Trebilcock. It concerns a dream related by William Dunstan, the carpenter and preacher of Hazeldene. He was going to Penelewey on business, walking along Tregie Road and down the steep hill to Come-to-good, when he met Mr Michael coming up, a man who had been dead several years. Mr Michael said 'I am going to Tregie to fetch Squire Penrose for it's time he came with us.' Next morning as he sat at breakfast Mrs Honor Wasley called him over the wall and told him 'Squire Penrose has gone, died sudden in the night.'

Houses at the crossroads

The shape of the roads was different in 1842 from now. Four roads converged on to the main road, in an irregular way with wide spaces and plots bulging into them. Houses were few: William Murton was at Victoria's Cottage next to the chapel, and had also fields and a building on the west side of Quenchwell road, Charles Trengrove and Henry Nicholls occupied Algarnick farm and a few fields to the north, and Henry Nicholls, carpenter and farmer, had one building on the site of Kiddleywink and fields on the east side of the main road. Broadway (previous name Gateshead), occupied by James Collins, stood between Tregie Road and F.P. 23 which was then the widest road of the four.

Above: Centre of Carnon Downs 1896. On the left is Datson's Corner. The wooden hut is the shop of Jonathan Penrose, shoemaker. John Mitchell was shopkeeper at Kiddleywink and is driving a horse and water barrel. The buildings on the right are smithy, carpenter's and Kiddleywink, and beside them is John Tippett, coachman, driving the Hon. John Boscawen's market waggon.

Shoemaker's hut in front of wall of Algarnick Farm. Quenchwell Road is on the left.

Kiddleywink Post Office

A carpenter's shop next to Kiddleywink remained into the 1930s, and the house became the village general stores. Whether it was ever a Kiddleywink cannot be proved; certainly it was not a beerhouse in living memory. Kiddleywinks, or beershops, were the consequence of an Act in 1830 which allowed any householder to buy for two guineas a licence to sell beer. The intention was to divert poor people from drinking gin which was legally obtainable only in public houses, and to help farmers by increasing the demand for barley. It was said that in some villages two out of three houses were beershops. Public houses, or inns, were meeting places for skittles and the reading aloud of newspapers, and provided for travellers. Kiddleywinks were cheaper competition and not inspected, and were accused of selling smuggled spirits and of hatching plots.

In the early 20th century the Mitchell family provided both food and water for the village. As a family they were carriers of heavy furniture, and of road stone from Devoran dock, by horse and cart. John and Mary Mitchell managed Kiddleywink as a shop, and John was also farming, milking and delivering milk, and carrying and delivering water. Their son Dickie took over the shop and the post office counter, and another son Billy Bell was a carpenter next-door.

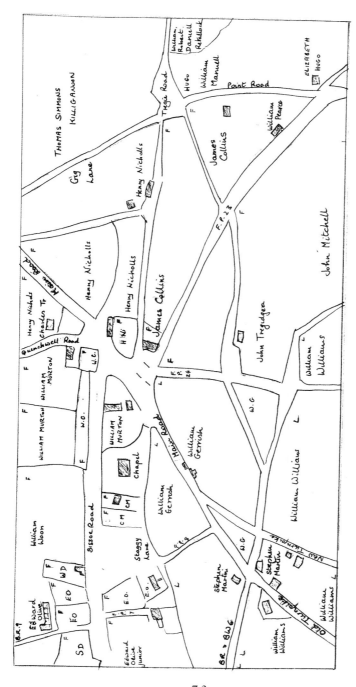

Middle of Carnon Downs 1842. Note shape of crossroads.
SD Stephen Dunstan, EO Edward Olive, WD William Dunstan, Tr Trengrove,
CM Charles Manuell, H Ni Henry Nicholls, WG William Gerrish, WC William Crowle,

73

Algarnick had more garden at the front than now, and opposite it on the corner of Quenchwell Road was a yard and cottage which became the home and store of Mr Datson who sold hardware and fuel by horse and cart. The cottage was demolished early in the 20th century.

The public road from the crossroads to Tresithick, F.P. 23, is the broadest road on the tithe map of Feock parish. It passed between Broadway (Gateshead) and its shed, on a paved embankment through fields and past a stable to Point Road, and along the footpath to Tresithick. The stable was let to William Pearce and shelters horses still. There was a William Pearce, a lead smelter, who died aged 80 at Gelidga (Clydia); could he be the same person? Much in history is guessing.

William Pearce's stable on footpath 23

Residents near the crossroads in 1842
Whom might you see if you stood there?

Edward Olive from Gerrans and living at Ebenezer had holdings in Bissoe Road: a house and and fields on the east side of the entrance to Heath Farm, a row of cottages at Trevince, and the plot and houses opposite, Ashtree.

Edward Olive senior held a Sunday school in his barn at Ebenezer and in 1825 founded the chapel. He was 56 in 1842, a cordwainer, and lived with his wife, son Samuel, 8, 4 daughters and a lodger, William

Bassett, also a shoemaker. In his eighties Edward was a collector of the Poor Rate, and two daughters, dressmaker and housekeeper, and William Bassett, were still living with him. Thomas Trebilcock recalls that one daughter married William Dunstan of Hazeldene and was the mother of Ralph Dunstan, musician, born in 1857.

William Dunstan, 25, of Hazeldene was a carpenter, builder and undertaker, and was affectionately recalled by Tom Trebilcock as a tireless and riveting preacher in his old age. His son was a wheelwright aged 15 in 1871 and his daughters became a grocer and a teacher while Ralph at 13 was a pupil teacher.

William Woon was the tenant of the field now Parc-an-Gwarry and northwards to beyond Valley Lane. He was a labourer from Roche, and later a lighterman, married to Christiana. His land was sold in 1920 to 'Lord' Burrell and was used for Sunday school treats.

A thin strip along the north side of Bissoe Road opposite the chapel was occupied by **William Crowle**, blacksmith, with his son Malachi, 14, blacksmith's apprentice, and his wife, younger son and 2 daughters. There is no building there on the map.

Charles Trengrove, 40, porter, was at Algarnick Farm with 3 children and Mary Ann, 30, dressmaker. In 1843, as a widower, he married Elizabeth Pengelley. His daughter Elizabeth Ann, a servant, married Thomas Tregaskis of Devoran. The elusive Nathaniel Trengrove, whether related I don't know, was a schoolmaster whose daughter Elizabeth Jane married another Pengelley, a railway porter, in 1864. Charles held three small fields between Main Road and Quenchwell Road.

Henry Nicholls held most of the land where 'The Forge'was built. In 1842 he was 43 with a wife, and a son aged 2. As well as his carpenter shop at Kiddleywink he had 2 houses on the north side of Tregie road. Large fields to the east of Chyreen and northwards to Playing Place were Walter Hearle's, leased from Thomas Simmons of Killiganoon.

James Collins held the fields on the south side of Tregie Road. He was a waterman, with wife and 3 children. He had Park Farm on Point

Road and the house now called Broadway, previously Gateshead. There was more space at the crossroads in 1842, and a village green where are now the entrances to the village hall and the hairdresser. F.P. 23 to Point Road and Tresithick was the widest track on the tithe map, and it still has granite posts and chains and is paved under the mud with quartz. The right of way was between Gateshead house and its shed.

Catherine Foster describes her childhood there in 1930:

She visited her great aunt and uncle Andrew. He was a miner from Durham and he had pneumoconiosis. She remembers the well outside the back door and the dreaded privy with wooden seat and bucket underneath, its contents being dug into the garden. Clem Jose was allowed to fetch water from the well. All and sundry walked through the front gate and and a field gate on their way to Point. She walked often to Penpol, picking flowers from the hedge.

John Tregidgea, 35, a grocer,with wife and 4 children, and George Tregidgea 35, tin miner, lived in the middle of Park View and held the fields on which the village hall was built.

William Murton, 40, carpenter, was at Crossways with his wife and 3 children. His tenancy had been agreed with the trustees of the chapel in 1825 and included a cottage and farm buildings at the junction of Bissoe and Quenchwell roads, later Mr Datson's cottage where he kept animals and from which he sold hardware and fuels from his horse and cart.

Charles Manuell likewise held land by agreement with chapel trustees. His patch, Aylesford, was to the west of the chapel as far as Staggy Lane, which was then wide open at the north end. He was 46, a porter, with 3 sons aged 16, 10, and 7, the eldest a miner, and a daughter.

The Wesleyan Chapel was the most prominent building and expanding. In 1842 it was extended at the west end to touch Mr Murton's stable, a stone hedge was built around it, and a gallery was built inside. Trees were planted in 1860 and before that it was starkly exposed at the crossroads among fields.

Gateshead (now Broadway)   Photos from Catherine Foster

Tregie Road

On the tithe map this road looks narrow and partly unfenced along waste land. Henry Nicholls of Algarnick and Kiddleywink held the fields on the north side halfway to Point Road and James Collins of Gateshead held the fields on the south side. On both sides of Gig Lane Daniell and Robert Retallack held fields, the same two brothers who farmed much of Tregie and were also at Ringwell. Also theirs were two unenclosed cottages in a layby at the east end of Henry Nicholls' land. James Collins had Park View Farm on Point Road, and the site of Park View bungalows was occupied by John Tregidgea, 35, a grocer, with a wife and 4 children, and Jane and Ann Gellard aged 70 and 34. John Tregidgea's holding included the triangular plot that 130 years later was sold by Mrs Roseveare for the village hall.

LORD FALMOUTH'S SALE

Only three months after Captain Tremayne's sale of land in 1920 the estates of the Right Honourable Evelyn Hugh John Viscount Falmouth were auctioned in the Concert Hall, Truro.

During the Great War the Cornwall Agricultural Committee was looking for increased production of food, particularly potatoes, both from farms and from new allotments. Young men departed and died, for instance William Davey, Willie Peters and John Bilkey. Postwar there was a shortage of young hardworking tenants, and a need for more independence and a more secure future for smallholders, and perhaps it was a relief for the big landowners to be no longer responsible for scattered patches of land. Both Viscount Falmouth and Captain Tremayne however reserved mineral rights:

> To ... is conveyed the field ... except 'all mines metals oil and minerals within and under the heredit ... together with all powers necessary for searching winning and disposing of same ... whether by underground or surface workings including power to let down the surface and to sink any pits or shafts or divert and use any waters or watercourses and to erect and construct any buildings engines roads railways tramways waterworks waterways airways

cables telegraphs telephones to stack any minerals and refuse which might be raised reasonable and proper compensation being paid to the purchaser.'

The description of the lots in Lord Falmouth's sale is a clue to home life in the early 20th century. Most were let on a yearly tenancy renewed at Michaelmas. Why were so many withdrawn from sale?

ESTATE OF RIGHT HONOURABLE VISCOUNT FALMOUTH
Valuable Freehold Properties
Auction September 1920

28   12 acres at Ringwell let to John Pengelley, rent £16.18.0 p.a. Old buildings, orchard, pasture, arable and waste. It was at the bottom of Ringwell campsite, 'The Valley'. No-one bid for it.

29   25 acres let to Nicholas Gay, rent £35 p.a. This is land east of Ringwell including Heath Farm. The house had sitting room, kitchen, back kitchen, dairy, pantry, coal house, two bedrooms, stable, linhay and loft over. There were also some buildings to the north next to the spring. Withdrawn from sale.

30   13 acres let to H C Burrell and W M Pengelley, house sublet to H M Burrows. Two sitting rooms, kitchen, dairy, 3 bedrooms. Cowhouse for 4 with loft over, meal house, furnace house, cart shed, apple house, two pigs' houses, calves' house. This is Trevilla, later occupied by Albert Hearn, retired smith. Withdrawn from sale.

31   7 acres let to F C Mitchell, house let to T Dunstan. Two stalls and a pig house. This land is on Quenchwell Road from Chyreen Lane to the well. The house is Satya, where Miss Peachey used to live. Withdrawn from sale.

32 11 acres let to H C Burrell, house sublet to J H Pengelley. Sitting room, kitchen, wood house, 2 bedrooms, boxroom. This is Ebenezer, once the home of Edward Olive. Withdrawn from sale.

33   8 acres let to H C Burrell and N J and W M Pengelley, rent £13. 15s.

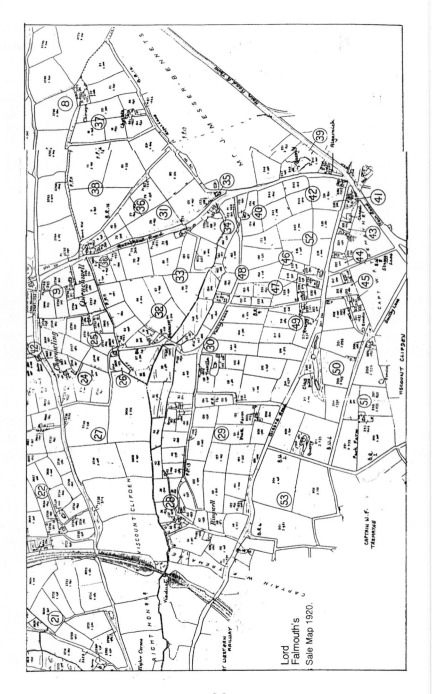

Lord
Falmouth's
Sale Map 1920.

House sublet to W J Verran. Cartshed, two-stall stable and loft over. This became the garden centre. Withdrawn from sale.

34 2 acres let to J. Dunstan. Cottage sublet to Misses Almond and Keir. Sitting room, kitchen, washhouse, 2 bedrooms, well. This must be where Misses Bowring and Philbrick started growing flowers and it is described in Feock Parish History book IV. The house was demolished and some of the land is in the garden centre. Withdrawn from sale.

35 Cottage occupied by G J Day. This is Algarnick or Halgarrick Cottage at the foot of Chyreen Lane. It is not on the tithe map so must have been built after 1842. Messer Bennett of Killiganoon bought it for £51.

36 7 acres of fields between Chyreen Lane and Quenchwell. House let to F C Mitchell. two-stall stable, cowhouse for three, barn, loosebox. Withdrawn from sale

37 5 acres let to to late N J Pengelley and W M Pengelley, rent £10. House sublet to A Field. Traphouse and Linhay. This is Chyreen. Withdrawn from sale.

38 11 acres let to J Dunstan, south-west of Chyreen. Withdrawn from sale.

39 4 acres let to W S Stanbury and J Mitchell. House sublet to William Dunstan. Two sitting rooms, kitchen, back kitchen, pantry, 3 bedrooms, boxroom, wash house and wood house. Pigs' house, cowhouse for 6 with barn over, calves' house, pigs' house. This is Algarnick Farm and it was bought by Messer Bennett, who already owned adjoining land between Chyreen Lane and the main road, for £420.

40 3 acres let to J Mitchell. Sitting room, kitchen, back kitchen, 2 bedrooms, wash house, calves' house, wood house and closet. This was William Woon's house in 1842 in Valley Lane. Withdrawn from sale.

41 One rood let to H C Burrell for £10 p.a. two sitting rooms, kitchen, dairy, 3 bedrooms wash house and loft over, stable, cowhouse for eight, cart shed. No tithes or taxes. This is Crossways/Victoria's between chapel

and Forth Coth, the same that was let to William Murton in 1842. Mr Burrell bought it for £250.

42 3 acres let to J Mitchell. Cottage sublet to to Mrs Pollard has sitting room, kitchen, 2 bedrooms. Cottage sublet to Mr Peters has sitting room, kitchen, 2 bedrooms, wood house, coal house, cart shed, calves' house, loft, traphouse, twostall stable and wood house. These are the cottages on Quenchwell Road opposite Algarnick Farm, which were later the home of Mr Datson with his horse and cart for selling hardware. The cottages were demolished. Withdrawn from sale.

43 3 roods let to H C Burrell and B Burrows, rent £4. 15. 0. Cottage sublet to W C Dunstan. Two sitting rooms, kitchen and two bedrooms, coalhouse adjoining. This is Aylesford, later the home of J Davey. W Dunstan bought it for £210.

44 2 roods let to B Burrows. Porch, sitting room, kitchen, pantry, two bedrooms, pig house, garden, field. This is Old Cottage, which did not exist in 1842. Ben Burrows bought it for £240.

45 1 acre let to J Davey for £9 p.a. Two cottages, each with sitting room, kitchen, 2 bedrooms, wash house, potato house. This is Ash Tree Cottage in Staggy Lane. Peter Hannam, brought up there, remembers it as three cottages in a row at right angles to the lane. It was his mother who started a post office in the main road in the 1930s. Mr Peters bought it for £255.

46 Three cottages let to W M Pengelley. Eight rooms, wood house and pig house sublet to W Baker. Four rooms and coal house sublet to S Allen. Two rooms and coal house sublet to Mrs Penaluna. No tithe or tax. This is Hazeldene, once the home of William Dunstan. W.M. Pengelley bought it for £300.

47 3 roods and 4 cottages let to W M Pengelley for £15 p.a., occupied by T White, T Coad, Mrs Tallack and Mrs Nicholls, each with 4 rooms and coal house and wood house. These are Rose and Lyn Cottages next to Hazeldene. W M Pengelley bought them for £300.

48 7 acres let to H C Burrell and W J Woolcock.   House occupied by

W J Woolcock. Sitting room, kitchen, dairy, 2 bedrooms, wash house, coal house, pigs' house. Well. This is Samaria. Withdrawn from sale.

49 5 acres let to W H Pengelley. Two cottages each have kitchen, sitting room and 2 bedrooms. One has a dairy. One cottage sublet to Mr Brabyn has sitting room, pantry, kitchen, store, and 2 bedrooms and wood house. Traphouse, coal house, wood house, potato house, calves' house, cowhouse for two, pony stable. Well. Quarry. This is Trevince. It was bought by William Henry Pengelley, a coachbuilder who worked in Calenick Street. He built carts and carriages in Calenick Street and cycled there daily. Later he was building 'Ranter' buses, coaches and ambulances. He was reputed to be a skilled and exacting tradesman and strict with his workers. During the second world war, when tractors were not allowed rubber for tyres, he invented wooden spade lugs which were sold countrywide by Ford and Truro Garage. His son Stan became a coach builder too, and his son Harry was a motor engineer and farmed. There were several Pengelley families in Carnon Downs. W.M. Pengelley was at Chyreen and has a memorial on the wall at Quenchwell chapel. Harry cannot remember whether they are related. Most marriages in Feock were between families in the same or next parish. Consequently there are more households than surnames. Admire Trevince, a Victorian small-holding, while it still stands.

50 17 acres let to J Woolcock for £18 p.a. House has 2 sitting rooms, kitchen, larder, 3 bedrooms, 2 boxrooms and dairy. 3-stall stable, cowhouse for 12, root house, chaff house tool house, calves' house, cart shed, furnace house, pigs' house, well, mowhay. This is the farm of George Knight, butcher and then of Clem Jose. At 50 Knight's Meadow was a Bronze Age tumulus. The house is still there, number 31, but the farm buildings have gone. The entrance to it became F.P.7. The field from Knights Meadow to the track at Croft Hill includes Lord Falmouth's waste land and was used as a claypit and quarry.

51 9 acres let to J Woolcock and Jane Burrows for £18.10.0 p.a. Two sitting rooms, kitchen, dairy, 3 bedrooms, box room. Pigs' house, furnace house, 2 pigs' houses, stable, cowhouse for four, barn, well. This is Park Farm, absent in 1842, when there were only some buildings now replaced by 22 Knights Meadow. John Tallack, water engineer at Bissoe, bought it

for £655. Its wide green meadows and peaceful herds are in one pair of hard-working hands to this day.

52   5 acres let to J Woolcock. This was four fields on the north side of Bissoe Road from opposite the chapel to Hazeldene. It was bought by Mr Burrell of Crossways/ Victoria's for £350. The Manse, Manse Road, and Whitehaven were built on it in the 1950s and '60s, leaving 3 acres of public open space owned by the County Council, which became Parc-an-gwarry.

53   11 acres let to J Woolcock. These are the fields between the Croft Hill track B.R.2 and the Ringwell Farm track B.R.4. There was no house, but in 1928 John Tallack built Croft Hill. Withdrawn from sale.

Presumably the 14 unsold lots were sold at a later date.

With the sales of the Lemon Carclew estate and Lord Falmouth's, landholding in Carnon Downs was transformed in 1920 from short insecure tenancies to a patchwork of freehold properties which could stay in the families for generations.

There was some land outside these estates: Treliever for instance was owned by a Hill family and parts of Carnon Crease by Hugo Warren and Enys. Thomas Simmons and his successor Messer Bennetts owned parkland on the north side of Tregie Road from Point Road to Come-to-good, and on both sides of the main road from Algarnick to the Kea boundary. Tregie remained Boscawen property, and Tresithick belonged to three Hugo sisters. These deserve separate chapters. There was also land in the Agar estate for which I have no record of the sale.

Carnon Crease

In the 1842 tithe map there is a patch on the south-west facing slope from Ringwell down to the Redruth and Chasewater Railway, and between Treliever and Carnon Wollas, called Carnon Crease. Part of it was then waste land. It was owned by Hugo Warren and Enys and sold in 1943 by Colonel Michell and Rev Enys. By then there were good tracks from Croft Hill on Bissoe Road and the mineral railway had gone.

1 8 acres occupied by G Pollard. 2 sitting rooms, kitchen, dairy, 2 bedrooms, boxroom, 2 linhay bedrooms, cowshed, 2 pigs' houses, fowls' house, cow house, barn. This is Keatreville or Catervilla, under the Falmouth railway viaduct. W Visick bought it for £600.

2 14 acres occupied by Mrs H Trebilcock, rent £38 p.a. 2 sitting rooms, back kitchen, 2 bedrooms, 2 linhay bedrooms, wash house, dairy with barn over, cow house for 7, fowls' house, bullocks' house, pigs' house, stable. This is Oak Farm and it was bought by Mr Barker for £650.

3 Cottage and one rood occupied by Miss Marshall for £4 p.a. Sitting room, kitchen, 2 bedrooms, outhouse, right to use well at lot 4. This was on the edge of the quarry below Oak Farm on F.P.5. It was bought by Miss Marshall for £150.

4 Cottage on one acre, occupied by Mr W Lean, rent £8 p.a. Sitting room, kitchen, scullery, 2 bedrooms, boxroom. Well. This is now a bungalow in an artistic garden in a quarry at the bottom of F.P. 5.

5 3½ acres occupied by T Barker, rent £20 p.a. 2 sitting rooms, kitchen, scullery, 2 bedrooms, boxroom. This is now White Cottage and Langford's flower farm on F.P.4. It was bought by Mr Barker for £455.

6 6 acres occupied by G Davey, rent £12 p.a. 2 sitting rooms, kitchen, scullery, 2 bedrooms, 2 linhay bedrooms, hay shed, wood shed, cart house, 3 pigs' houses. This is Croft Farm on B.W.6. It was bought by G Davey.

THE LAND of LANHYDROCK

Richard Robartes, from a family of merchants and bankers concerned with tin, was knighted and bought Lanhydrock in 1620. His son built the house, fought for Oliver Cromwell, lost the house to Sir Richard Grenville, and yet his descendents acquired land in the county and beyond and, rich from mineral rights, financed Redruth hospital, contributed to the cathedral, and rebuilt houses on their estates. One of their enterprises was Devoran, bought in 1829 from Samuel Hugo for £3800 (CL52). The records about the new town, and particularly the 19th century letters of the agent Alfred Jenkin, bring to life the hopes and anxieties of the time, the slippery roads, the drains, the uncertain harvests, the search for stone.

In 1842 the Robartes family owned Middle Devoran Farm, Wellington Place and the land south of there between Old Carnon Hill and the turnpike, and some fields to the west side of Old Carnon Hill. The names Agar and Clifden are reminders of Lanhydrock. Anna Maria Agar had inherited the estate.

How that happened was that a female Robartes married George Hunt and their daughter Anna Maria married Charles Agar Viscount Clifden. It was their son Thomas Agar Robartes who provided Redruth Hospital. His son Thomas Charles became Viscount Clifden in his turn and some time early in the 20th century must have sold his lands in Carnon Downs. Agar Farm on the west side of Old Carnon Hill was bought by Mr Lilly, and in the 1920s bungalows were built above and below on both sides of the road.

Wellington Place

Wellington Place, home of Thomas Martin.
   ⊗   is the site proposed as a gunpowder store in 1849.
The branch of byeway 1 from Wellington Place to opposite Devoran Lane did not exist in 1842

See pages 156 &158 for the gunpowder store.

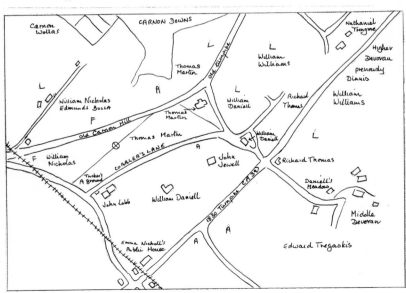

In 1850 Anna Maria Agar leased land to John Wellington for £2.15.0 p.a. on the lives of his children Bryan, Christian and John, 'except parts of common tin copper lead and clay stones and liberty to dig and carry and ways and watercourses and liberty to carry away water and trees and lops and shreds'. There were several families of Wellingtons in Feock at the time. The tithe map shows a house at Wellington Place, fields to the south and on the opposite side of Old Carnon Hill occupied by Thomas Martin, the road F.P.1 to Lower Clydia, and the road B.W.1 downhill to the line of the Redruth and Chasewater Railway.   (CL54)

Gunpowder Plot

More detail is to be found on a map made in 1849 (CL Box 319). This is a proposal to store gunpowder on the Agar field leased to Thomas Martin to the west of Cobblers' Lane. The site is now North Grange Industries.

The object of the map is to count the number of people living within range of the gunpowder store. Old Carnon Hill (Old Turnpike) is 5 chains away to the west, Cobblers' Lane the same distance to the east. At the bottom of the lane were 2 houses containing 13 people; one of the houses was Spring Vale where lived Thomas Lobb the gardener and collector of plants. Further up was William Daniell's house with 8 inhabitants, and at the top was Wellington Place, 10 chains from the store. Lower Clydia and Oak Tree Cottage at the entrance to Middle Devoran were 5 chains further. The lane B.W.1 which crosses the main road to Devoran Lane, and which was not drawn on the 1842 tithe map, is shown and immediately north of it is 'Jewell's Villa', now White Lodge. Surveyors used metal chains, each 22 yards long and made of 100 links. Storage of gunpowder was a recurrent scare in Devoran, and an empty field on Agar land on the outskirts was a possible solution.

Railway

The rules for the Devoran quay, sluice pond and the Redruth & Chasewater Railway as far as Carnon Bridge through Agar land are preserved in a book of 88 brittle brown pages dated 1824, and cover compensation to residents, George Rouse and Samuel Stephens for instance, through whose garden and orchard the railway would pass, rights of the company to build and to carry, and the denial of any right to the company to minerals underground. Charges for carriage by the railway were listed, 2d per ton per mile for sand and dung, metals, coal and stone, 3d for earth, 4d for grain. (CL 335)

School

The censuses of 1851 onwards state the occupation of some children aged two to twelve as 'scholars'. In the first half of the century children were taught at home, or by neighbours, and in the Wesleyan Sunday school. There were small dame schools, it is said, in the room above the chapel stable, in the loft at Trerise, and in the back room of Lower Clydia. In 1847 the vicar and churchwardens of Feock agreed to buy from Thomas James Agar Robartes a piece of waste ground, 30 perches bounded on two sides by roads, 'minerals excepted with liberty to search, break and carry away ... to be used for a school for the education of children and adults or children only of labouring, manufacturing and other poorer classes and as residence for schoolmaster or mistress.' The minister of Feock Parish was to appoint a master or mistress and management was to be by a committee of minister, curate, Earl of Falmouth, Thomas James Agar-Robartes and Gilbert of Trelissick, 'as long as these are members of the Church of England and have an interest in estate in the parish' and subscribe 20/- p.a. (CL Box 319)

Nearly 10 years later Devoran church was built. The new turnpike had been opened in the eighteen thirties, so that Carnon Downs people could easily walk both to church and to school on a road instead of through the fields via Point and Narabo. Carnon Downs was not yet a village but a scattering of settlements enclosed from waste in the western fringe of Feock and then Devoran parishes. What it did have before either the school or the church was built on Agar land in Devoran was the chapel, founded in 1825, and enlarged in 1842 by an addition at the west end and a gallery, to provide 537 sittings of which 133 were sold to their occupants.

Middle Devoran Farm

Lanhydrock documents refer to Devoran Cock which may include Middle Devoran which was the piece of Agar estate immediately south of Earl Falmouth's Higher Devoran, and north of Devoran church. Until the new turnpike cleaved it it was in continuity with Wellington Place, and Jewell's Villa. Edward Tregaskis was the main tenant in 1842, holding land on both sides of the new turnpike. Three houses are drawn on the tithe map, with an entrance from the turnpike and a road, now F.P.25, linking it to Higher Devoran and to Devoran church. At the main road, north side of the entrance, was also Oak Tree cottage on Lemon land and let to Richard Thomas, and there was

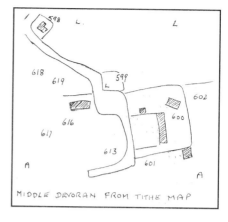

MIDDLE DEVORAN FROM TITHE MAP

another enclosure on the north side of the lane and on Lemon land, called Daniell's Meadow. Today Higher and Middle Devoran are farmed by the same family and there is an array of farm buildings both new and old, one stone one still equipped as a killing house but not in use.

TRESITHICK
Tresedeck. Farm of the arrow?

The settlement of Tresithick is haunted by two ladies whose names appear as landowners on the 1842 tithe map list. The freehold of most of Tregie's land was owned by Juliana Penrose and Lord Falmouth and the latter owned also the fields on both sides of the Point Road. But there were houses and fields in their midst that were both owned and occupied by Elizabeth and Martha Hugo. Where Paula Blake lived in the 20th century, 'Tangye', was owned by Elizabeth, as was Tresithick House, later the home of Norman Dunstan, who provided an annexe for Frank and Hetty Trebilcock. Opposite Tangye in Tresithick Lane is 'The Cottage', home until the 1990s of Miss Philbrick, generous secretary of our Old Cornwall Society and writer about roads and packet ships; in 1842 it was leased to Martha from Lord Falmouth. Jointly Elizabeth and Martha owned 'Higher Tresithick', known to our generation as George Roberts' farm with 39 acres and a wind pump. Further east Elizabeth owned 19 acres including a couple of 'poor fields and moor', and also the furthest house on the south side of the lane. The tenants of the fields were William Manuell, Henry Libby, John Trenhaile and the farmer of Killiganoon, Walter Hearle.

By 1920 Higher and Lower Tresithick were the property of the Boscawen family and included in the sale of Tregie. No Hugos were mentioned. Who were these ladies who mysteriously acquired houses and land and then faded away?

Miss Philbrick, living as she did with Martha's ghost, diligently searched parish registers and discovered an interested Hugo in Maidstone. Her correspondent as it happened was descended from Peter Hugo, brother of Richard, the father of Elizabeth and Martha. Richard had five children: Juliana born in 1761, Martha 1763, Elizabeth 1766, Richard 1768 and Stephen 1770. His grandfather came from Saint Just-in-Roseland and is called in the family tree 'Richard of Trevilla'. He appears in the Feock marriage register in 1760.

Richard could have left his property to any of his five children, all of them single, but at the time of the tithe map Juliana, Stephen and Richard were dead, leaving Martha and Elizabeth aged 79 and 77 alone in their houses without any close family. By 1846 they were both dead and buried

Tresedeck in 1842

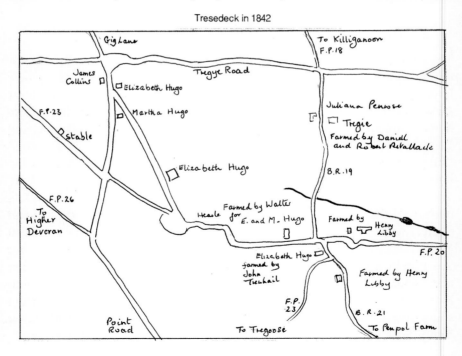

in Feock and the family line was at an end. The Maidstone Hugo finds that Elizabeth's estate, mainly land, was willed to her cousin's son Richard who lived at Golla. Presumably he sold the property because he emigrated to Guernsey and there joined his uncle Samuel, who had lost money invested in mines, learnt dentistry, made a good living by it, and offered hospitality to all his young relations, some of whom succeeded him as Guernsey dentists.

Peter Hugo meanwhile was buying Devoran Cock in 1804 before it was industrialised, that is before the railway, the dock, and the new town, when it was farm and common. (CL50)

Martha and Elizabeth, in their late seventies in 1842, let their many acres to farmers: Walter Hearle at Higher Tresithick, and John Trenhaile at Lower Tresithick south side where his fields were called Mowhay, Barn Meadow, Homer Great Close, Gleaner, Coppice. The other cottage at Lower Tresithick north side was Lord Falmouth's and had culver house, Great Close and waste let to Henry Libby.

The ways to Tresithick

The approach to Tresithick was on the tithe map the widest road in Feock parish, and led from Gateshead, now Broadway, between house and shed, across fields on a raised and metalled embankment, past William Pearce's stable where two horses still live, to Point Road and onward into Tresithick. John Tregidgea had a house and fields where Park View now is, and James Collins of Gateshead had Park View Farm. The track is now F.P.23 alongside the village hall and across Park View, interrupted by the 1991 bypass and resumed on the other side of it.

Six roads, now public footpaths, converged on these cottages and farms, connecting them with their farming neighbours and the sea. Tresithick Lane forks from Point Road and passes Tresithick house, joins F.P.23, turns eastwards, passes Higher Tresithick farm and reaches the two farmhouses of Lower Tresithick. From here there are 4 divergent paths all requiring wellington boots in wet weather. B.R.19 turns north across a stream to Tregie. F.P.20 descends beside the water gardens of Tregie and through abandoned soft fruit fields and across the stream to

F.P.33 which joins Come-to-good to Harris Hill Foot at Penpol. B.R.21 leads through a slate cutting and woods to Penpol Farm. F.P. 22 wanders through wood and field to Tregoose.

In 1921 when Lady Margaret Boscawen sold Tregie, Tangye and Tresithick house were not included because they belonged to Mrs Dunstan. All of Higher and Lower Tresithick farms, some 85 acres, were in the sale as part of the grounds of Tregie:

Higher Tresithick had 'cowhouses for 6 and 7, feeding passages and barn over, root house, calves' house and 4-bay cart shed'.

Lower Tresithick had 'a modern house, coal house and wash house in garden, and a cottage, yearlings' house, 3 loose boxes and loft over, 2 pigs' yards, 2 loose boxes with barn over, root house, meal house, store and chicken house'.

'The stock raised and the dairy produce have secured many distinctions in the showyard.' (WH6453)

TREGIE
Tregye Treguy Tregy
Farm with a dog?

A study of this estate was published in the Feock Local History Group's part III in 1975. It is out of print but a few treasured copies exist and it can be borrowed from the Courtney Library. In the same book are copied the inventories of brothers Stephen and William Adams of Tregie in 1719 and 1725, that is a valuation by two friends of their property at the time of death. Here is William's, 'appraised by ... Hopson Woolcock', a name connected with Ringwell Farm:

	£	s
Purse and wearing apparrell	3	0
Chattle Estate in Tregy	100	0
Two cows £4 and 3 small heifers £2.10	6	10
A young mare	1	10
for 10 sheep at home and 3 sheep abroad	2	0
for 5 lambs at home and 2 lambs abroad	0	14

for bees at home and abroad	1	1
Two acres of barley	3	0
for bedding	10	0
Three silver spoons and a silver taster	1	0
A Cyder Beame and one Harrow	1	0
two Hogsheads and five halfe hogsheads	1	0
potts and brass	1	0
an old cart and an old gun	0	12
pewter and Court Cupboard and irons and spit	2	0
A round table and two side tables and a form	1	0
Eleven chaires and a dozn and halfe of glass bottles		17
for wooll	1	0
for debts sparate and desparate	45	0
for things forgotten and unappraised	1	10

William left his part of Tregie to his daughter Ann, but by 1800 Lord Falmouth was selling Tregie land, 13½ acres on the north side of Tregie Road, to Thomas Spry of Killiganoon, and in 1807 John Libby left his leasehold Tregie land to his nephew William Penrose. He married Juliana Roberts of Lamellyn in 1814 and their son was born in 1821. Tragically he died in 1838 and his son was drowned 4 years later. On a wall in Feock parish church is a marble tablet with this inscription:

'Sacred to the memory of William Penrose Esquire of Tregye in this parish who died suddenly on 28 March 1838. An affectionate husband and father, a kind friend and benevolent neighbour, he lived distinguished and when it pleased the creator to end his term of days he died sincerely lamented. To the memory of William Roberts Penrose Esquire, only son of the above named who in the prime of his life was accidentally drowned by the upsetting of a boat at the entrance to Truro River on 2 July 1842 in 22nd year of his age. His amiable manners had endeared him to an extensive circle of acquaintances by whom his loss was most sincerely deplored and his untimely decease which cast a mournful gloom over the minds of his surviving friends, is here most affectionately recorded by his sorrowing mother, Juliana Penrose. She died 8 June 1850.'

The estate was let:

'Tregie house, stables, coach-house, labourer's cottage, 5 acres of orchards, 54 acres of excellent arable and pasture, and tenement of Come-to-good.' The house 'pleasantly situated in a garden, has a southern aspect and commands views of Falmouth harbour. Comprises cheerful dining room, drawing room, breakfast parlour and book room, 2 kitchens, 6 bedrooms, dairy, pantry, beer, cider and wine cellars, apple house with cider press. Walled garden stocked with choice of fruit trees, orchards in full bearing, greenhouse.'

Inscribed over the front door is 'W.P. 1805'.

All 54 acres were leased to William Retallack and sons Robert and Daniell, while the mansion house, walled gardens, orchard and labourer's cottage were let separately. The tithe map states that Juliana Penrose owned 30 acres while the rest was leased to her by Lord Falmouth. The field names are listed eg Post Meadow, Long Moor, Higher Beef Close, Well Close, Barn and Mowhay, Hicks Meadow, and, with a hint of prehistory, Gear. Gear in Cornwall usually means camp and the southern border of this field on the slopes below modern Tregye Meadow is curved on the map so that is tempting to complete a circle and imagine a prehistoric round.

Living at Tregie in 1842 were Rev. Francis Cole, vicar of Feock, with his wife, son, 3 daughters and 2 young servants, John and Hannah. In the cottage were Samuel Mortimer, 25, gardener, and Norman, 12. In 1844 Rev. Cole moved to St Issey. The 1851 census lists no residents at all for the mansion. A cottage is occupied by John Roberts, lead smelter, and his wife and sons; Richard was a shoemaker, John a lead smelter, and William aged 11 an agricultural labourer; there were 4 other children aged 14 to 2. Another was occupied by William Woolcock, agricultural labourer, with his wife and 4 children aged 7 years to 3 months.

Ten years later Tregie at last became a family home again. William Retallack had died and Robert moved to Trevilla, leaving Daniell, 57, farming 88 acres. He had acquired a wife, Sarah, 38, and with her a daughter-in-law Catherine, 12, described as house servant, and Elizabeth, 16, farm servant. In a cottage were Thomas and Mary Barrett, farm labourer and washerwoman, and their grandson, 11, farm labourer. This small working team kept house and fields. Sarah lived at Tregie for 30 years.

Some clues to her life can be traced in marriage registers and censuses:

In 1848 Nicholas Tallack, waterman of Narabo, married Sarah Gerrish daughter of William Gerrish, mason of Carnon Downs. The census records 4 daughters of William Gerrish, the eldest aged 20 in 1848 and none of them called Sarah. Perhaps Sarah was already living away from home before she married.

In the 1851 census: at Narabo Nicholas Tallack, 33, waterman, wife Sarah, 28, and Catherine, 2.

In 1859 there were two marriages in the Gerrish family. James Michell married Emily, and Daniell Retallack, farmer of Tregie, married Susan Tallack, widow, both ladies being daughters of William Gerrish. Could Susan be Sarah?

In 1861 Daniell Tallack died. 31 acres of Tregie were sold.

In 1864 John Dunstan farmer married Sarah Retallack of Tregie, daughter of William Gerrish.

In 1871 census: at Tregie were John Dunstan, 35, farmer of 85 acres, his wife Sarah, 48, said to be from Perranarworthal, Catherine, 22, and a servant. There were 7 other adult residents on the estate, farm labourers, a blacksmith apprentice, and a sailor, and there were at least 10 small children.

Sarah had stayed at Tregie after her husband Daniell died and some of his land was sold, perhaps to Lord Falmouth. But the farm was saved when she married John Dunstan, a farmer from Kea 13 years younger than herself, and employing a man and 2 boys on 85 acres. Sarah died in 1886, and John in 1889 aged 54.

Top three photos: Tregye, house and garden at the time of the 1921 sale

Bottom: Boys' Brigade tea treat at Tregye, 1910. Lady Margaret pours tea and Hon. John Boscawen stands on steps

Twentieth century and Happy Valley

Big changes were waiting to happen. The 6th Viscount Falmouth died and Tregie became the home of his youngest son, Honorable John Richard de Clare Boscawen together with his new wife Lady Margaret, daughter of the Earl of Strafford. Feock Local History part III describes the alterations, cottages at the entrance, and the creation of Happy Valley water gardens, which are still visible from F.P.20, a series of pools and tropical-looking trees and giant rhododendrons. Yellow lilies from there have floated down-river and thrive at Penpol. Luckily the great grand-daughter of William Pearce, stone mason at Tregie and one of its oldest employees, remembers a description in the *West Briton* of the homecoming of Lord and Lady Petre (Hon. John and Lady Margaret Boscawen?) in 1913 when William Pearce led the cheers. By then the house had been enlarged with a second storey under a pitched roof. The photograph which I mistakenly labelled Killiganoon in *House on a Heath* is of the south face of Tregie with Hon. John and Lady Margaret treating the Boys Brigade to tea on trestle tables. My mistake was because the south face has been covered by a flat-roofed extension.

Hon. John with Rev. Arthur Boscawen established the Spring Flower Show and was its secretary. He died in 1915 and after the Great War Tregie was the home of Mr and Mrs Edward Rogers. Mrs Rogers enriched the gardens with plants brought from expeditions financed by her family, the Williams of Burncoose and Caerhays. She lived at Tregie until the second world war when armed forces displaced her. She is remembered for giving boots to children at Christmas and for paying for electricity to be relayed to a few houses 30 years before Carnon Downs had mains electricity.

Mr Len Wilde was one of those armed forces and happily remembered red squirrels in the yew trees, grass snakes slithering on the lawn, and Happy Valley beyond the orchard where medlar apples grew, hydrangeas lining the drive, sweet chestnuts, a tawny owl perched on a tree in daylight, and open view to the Carrick Roads. Mr Wilde was with Company 205 Field Ambulance R.A.M.C., whose soldiers could be hired to work for farmers, and Mr Vinden taught him to cultivate violets. He remembers Mrs Rogers visiting the house, and spent happy hours with the gardener George Lilley.

Lady Margaret Boscawen sold Tregye in 1921, soon after the sales of Falmouth and Lemon lands, presumably to Mrs Rogers. The description sounds magnificent:

Lot 1

Tregye house and Grounds
Well equipped Home Farm
Model dairy and farm homestead
Forming a Gentleman's residence and pleasure farm
160 acres

The residence is approached by a pretty carriage drive between specimen trees and contains

Ground floor: vestibule and hall with oak parquet floor, octagonal drawing room, dining room with large bay, library, boudoir, study, W.C., lavatory (H & C), pantry with plate safe, passage, servants' hall, kitchen, scullery, dairy, larder, coals, servants' W.C., and boot hole. Three staircases to

First floor: 5 bedrooms, dressing room, night nursery, day nursery, bathroom (H & C), W.C., housemaid's sink.

Second floor: 4 bedrooms, W.C., linen room (heated), workroom, boxroom, housemaid's sink.

Basement: Wine cellar, store, game cellar, heating apparatus.

The residence is substantially built of stone with slated roof, and heated by hot water radiation. It is 300 feet above sealevel with a south aspect and commands views of Carrick Roads and St. Anthony Point.

Stabling

is on north-west of residence and comprises: large coach house for 3, harness room with loft over, three-stall stable, 2 loose boxes with loft over, garage with inspection pit and heated by hot water pipes, yard with water laid on from reservoir.

Some entries in the marriage register 1850s and 1860s are a clue to the ownership of Killiganoon thereafter. Of Thomas Simmons' daughters:

Eliza married Charles James Bennetts, surgeon of Tregony.

Mary married Robert Michell merchant of Devoran.

Jane Messer Simmons married John Blarney accountant of St. Clement.

John the solicitor's clerk may have died young. In Feock church, Mr Hobba said in a lecture, is a memorial to John Messer Simmons who died age 24 in 1855. His brother, Thomas Davy, was then 12, and appears in a document of 1869. (WH1397)

Incidentally some employees at Killiganoon were marrying at this time:
Elizabeth Jane daughter of Henry Gregor, agricultural labourer at Killiganoon, married George Samsin servant at Killiganoon.

Band of Hope at Killiganoon

Thomas Gregor, labourer at Killiganoon, married Eliza Ann daughter of Nathaniel Trengrove schoolmaster of Carnon Downs.

According to the 1871 census there were over 100 people living at Killiganoon in 24 households. Thomas Simmons was still there. Other residents were William Jose a groom, 6 agricultural labourers, a porter, a woodman, 3 sawyers and a farmer, all of whom could have been employed on the estate. Others had jobs outside: a porter, mariner, undertaker, grocer, brakeman, railway porter, vitriol worker. Some of the wives and daughters, even as young as 15, are described as housekeepers. There were 54 children aged 12 and under, most of them scholars. The undertaker was William Dunstan, 10 years ago at Hazeldene, with his wife Ann and daughter Emily a grocer, daughter Ellen a teacher, and Ralph the future musician a pupil teacher.

It is a puzzle where they all lived. The house was rebuilt after a fire in 1872 and the estate came to John Messer Bennetts, presumably the son of Charles and Eliza. He farmed and gardened until he sold it before World War II. It has been since then a hotel, and several private residences. Land on the west side of the main road has been sold separately, lately becoming The Forge and a new plantation. Some of Walter Hearle's fields are Carnon Downs Caravan Park. There are still trees. Although many grand old oaks were felled when the A39 and Gig Lane were widened, there were new trees planted beforehand around the campsite. One field in Tregye Road has been preserved as a sports field shared with Truro College. One feature in its east hedge was particularly noted by Tom Trebilcock's mother who remembered that the mound there, now an untidy heap of branches and discarded metal and wood crowned with oaks, was once a beacon where a bonfire was lit at the time of the Spanish Armada. There is also a tumulus marked there on O.S. map 1880. The woods can be seen across the Come-to-good valley from F.P. Kea 14 (turn north immediately east of the Quaker chapel).

Signs in stone

The granite 3-mile-stone between Carnon Downs and Playing Place is placed close to Killiganoon hedge. The 4-mile-stone is on Old Carnon Hill, the turnpike road to Perranwell until 1830. It is possible that before about 1700 Killiganoon fields on both sides of the present A39 were in continuity and the track to Perranwell and to Bissoe from Truro was along B.R.14 and 15 past Chyreen to Higher Carnon.

Another granite relic stands wreathed in ivy and bramble in the southernmost hedge of Killiganoon, opposite Tregie entrance and about 25 metres further uphill. On this one is engraved 'S' on the west side and 'RS' on the east side. A guess would be 'S' for Simmons or Spry and 'RS' for Retallack or Rogers.

News from *West Briton*

The following reports were published in the *West Briton*. Some were selected by R.M. Barton and published in 1970 by D. Bradford Barton Ltd in *Life in Cornwall in the 19th Century*.

1835 'Pilchards are put with vinegar and bay leaves in earthenware vessels. The glaze is vitriolized lead and acid makes it poisonous. Bat leaves are a species of laurel which is poisonous.'

1843 'Margaret Nicholls said "I live at Quenchwell and I was going to Devoran to wash at 15 minutes past 5 in the morning. It was dark and wet and I had my umbrella up. My next-door neighbour put one hand on my eyes and one on my mouth and put his leg in front and tripped me over. I had money in a calico bag, 2 knobs of sugar, a thimble and a key." Prisoner sentenced to be transported.'

1844 '150-200 boats may be seen on a fine day engaged in oyster fishery in Falmouth Harbour. Fishermen are making little fortunes.'

1847 'Families are known to subsist on scarcely any other food than turnips fried with the tallow of miners' candles.'

1848 'The average age of all who died in the Truro District was 33 years.'

1865 'Elizabeth Evans of Bissoe Pool summoned Richard Burrows who had entered her house, caught her by the throat and brandished a stick. He said "I thought she was a witch and had ill-wished me."'

1866 'Severe storm. Railway blocked by fall of telegraph poles and wires entangled.'

1866 'Opening of broad gauge system from London to Mounts Bay. The impetus it will give to the produce of fisheries and market gardens is recognised.'

1868 Fear of bread riots.

1869 'Immense shoal of pilchards from Lizard to Eddystone.'

1870 R.M. Barton writes: 'Waste land was being cultivated. North Cliffs were set on fire. Lord Falmouth gradually enclosed his waste land. Often the poor and destitute and out-of-work miners were employed to burn furze, blast and remove rock, build walls, level and drain. Some waste land was set aside for gardens and recreation.'

1870 'Beerhouses losing their licences have to close.'

1878 'James Davy, rag and bone gatherer, fined 5/- and costs for striking with a stick Ann Dunstan and her son James who were coming from Carnon Downs into Truro by donkey cart. Davy said the boy called him names.'

TAMING THE HEATH

In the spring when fields are bright with dense green grass, when blackbirds collect wisps of hay and a robin sings on the peak of a hawthorn in early leaf, when hedges are white with sloe, and tiny pink flowers dot the dark holly leaves, when there are bluebells under oak trees and primroses in the crevices of walls, then Carnon Downs is impressive in its fertility. Camellias and azalias bloom red and pink and white, while daffodils are already seeding, and last year's barley fields have been ploughed and sown. Shrubs rise to new life, cabbage and broccoli are cut and gone and there are leeks and onions in their place. New lambs bleat at Come-to-good, sheep roam at Dower Ruth, horses at Heath Farm and a donkey at The Croft. Through autumn and winter there were herds of cattle on Carnon Crease, and fields of flowers. It is a picture of abundance.

Yet for centuries this area was a wild heath, and to wild heath it returns when it is neglected. Gorse grows 3 metres high in a year or two on high places, and reeds, rushes and willows on the low. Brambles scramble over gardens untended for even only a few months, lawns sprout docks and hawkweeds, celandines and strawberries creep over paths and flowerbeds, campions and stitchwort in the hedgerows.

When the bypass was being excavated the underlying rock was exposed. It is yellow/brown slate in friable slabs alternating with sticky buff clay and stained with layers of iron oxide. The layers are sometimes horizontal, sometimes upheaved to nearly vertical. Both the clay and the slate are impervious to water and hard to dig, the clay being clinging when wet and baked hard when dry, and the slate needs a pick to break it. But 200 years of carrying and spreading manure and compost have succeeded in making topsoil, and the presence of springs of water and rivers in the valley bottoms have made cultivation possible.

A witness from the reign of Queen Elizabeth I

Richard Carew, who described Cornwall as he saw it in 1602, wrote: 'In times past the Cornish people gave themselves ... to the seeking of tin, and neglected husbandry. As for tillage, it came far short of feeding the inhabitants' mouths, who were supplied weekly at markets. But when the tinworks began to fail and the people to increase this double necessity drove them to play the good husbands and to provide corn of their own. Yet whosoever looketh into the endeavour which the Cornish husbandman is driven to use about his tillage shall find the travail painful, the time tedious, and the expenses chargeable. About May they cut up all the grass of that ground which must be newly broken into turfs. These they raise up that the wind and sun may dry them. The husbandman pileth them in little heaps and so burneth them to ashes.'

Carew continues: 'They bring in sacks of sand, 120 sacks per acre. Before ploughing they scatter abroad those sand heaps, which afterwards, by the plough's turning down, give heat to the root of the corn. The tillable fields are in some places so hilly that the oxen can hardly take sure footing, some so tough that the plough will scarcely cut them, some so shelfy that the corn hath much ado to fasten his root. This done the tiller can commonly take but two crops of wheat and two of oats and then is driven to give it 7 or 8 years leyre and to make his breach elsewhere.

'Barley is grown into great use ... and of this the poor found benefit ... fed by the bread thereof. They carry their barley to the mill within 8 or 9 weeks from the time that they sowed it.'

In 1794 Robert Fraser described the land of Cornwall in *A view of Cornwall for the consideration of the board of Agriculture*:

'The internal parts of the county present immense tracts of uncultivated wastes and undivided commons and excepting mining districts almost without inhabitants.' The mines, he says, support 60,000 people as well as merchants and artisans and seamen, and miners are better paid than other labourers, and are the market for farm produce.

He comments: 'the gentlemen' eg Sir Francis Bassett 'encourage farmers to pick out quartz and to add granite debris.'

Miners have time on their hands, he says, and spend it looking for fuel. Much waste oozy bogland could be cultivated. Mr Praed has levelled heaps of stones and let earth and mud from mills run over them, and has grown hay and made pasture for sheep. Slaty earth, he says, is good enough for wheat and barley.

'West Cornwall cannot grow enough corn for the population, whereas nearer Devon a surplus is exported. Almost annually there are risings in protest' (the protest being against the export of grain to England or even abroad, while Cornish miners went hungry).

'Husbandry was little practised 200 years ago. Ground was all common or divided by stichemeal.'

'The people are devoted to tin.'

The usual sequence of arable cultivation, observed Fraser, was: Sow wheat, barley or oats for as long as it will bear, then grass for 10 years, then corn again. The exhausted land becomes furze. It is then necessary to 'Pare and burn the ground, scatter ash and compost of sand and scrapings from lanes, and straw and dung from farmyards or bought in towns. Fetch sand on horses or mules, 100 horseloads per acre. Chop wheat seed in with mattock, and next year barley and oats, adding ryegrass, trefoil and Dutch clover with the last crop. The best farmers grow only one crop of barley then grass for 4 years and add dung and earth. After wheat turnips can be sown with dung and sand, and then barley and grass.' But, he says, most farmers exhaust their land.

A ploughing team is 2 - 4 oxen, led by horses and a man or boy. The Cornish plough is awkward and Society of Agriculture will introduce Suffolk ploughs. Quartz stones are dug up from 20 inches deep, which would be better done by hacking and trenching. Cornwall has vast numbers of little horses and mules which are turned onto common and so cost nothing.

The compost of the best farmers is sea sand, dung, rotten slate and decayed pilchards declared unfit to eat and sold for 1/- per bushel.

Turnips, he says, need weeding and the farmers don't do it.

Potatoes can be dug in May and a second crop planted. 'The strongest men and the most beautiful women are found in Ireland where the principal food is potato' says Dr Smith. Potatoes cannot be preserved and they are heavy, so are grown in small quantities. They can usefully be fed, steamed, to bullocks, sheep, hogs and horses.

Fraser advises that sheep, cattle and horses should graze grass, thereby manuring it. Cornish cows are small with little flesh. Devon ones are better. They are kept mainly for calving, and kept indoors all winter on a stone foundation with cob walls.

Mules are for mining and priced at £18 each. Horses are small and hardy for carrying and dragging. No carts are used.

Sheep from Dorset, Devonshire and Leicester are better than Cornish ones.

Only a third of Cornwall is cultivated, leaving the rest waste. Big landowners let small plots to tenants who may cultivate them profitably.

Oak, ash, elm and plane have been planted by Sir John St. Aubyn and cider apples do well in the east.

Cut corn is built into arrish-mows, cones 12 feet high, beards inwards, with a sheaf on top, then by some farmers built into ricks in the yard. Clover and hay are stacked between layers of straw.

Fraser recommends that miners and fishermen should cultivate little farms, and the government should offer premiums for cattle and sheep and fences and draining. He points to tithes as an obstacle because they are subject to argument; the value of money declines and the clergy have to be kept. He hopes that the gentlemen will exert themselves for the benefit of the county.

So concluded Fraser. Half a century later the report was little better.

'Unless you advance you must necessarily go backwards.'

Karkeek, writing his report on farming in Cornwall in 1846, asks why the intelligence and experience which has so improved mining has not been applied to farming. Still most of the land is waste and only 1/10 of the inhabitants work on farms, most of which are small and ill-managed.

Springs break forth in winter, and in summer if the lie of slate is horizontal the thin soil is too dry. Few green crops are grown, vetches and carrots are poor, sainfoin and lucerne are experimental, swedes a novelty. White turnips are common but not properly seeded and weeded. They are good for feeding cattle, causing them to make more manure, which improves corn crops. Cattle are few, about 20 per hundred acres. After 3 years in pasture fields can grow potatoes, turnips, wheat and barley in succession. But wheat in south Cornwall is expensive to grow, requiring ploughing, harrowing, and spreading burnt weeds, and lime and dung. Barley cultivation costs half as much.

Earl Falmouth has tackled the reclamation of waste land by leasing 3 - 5 acre pieces to miners at a rent of 4/- per acre and on condition that the tenant builds a cottage there. Manure and bone and guano are needed. The first crop, turnips, is eaten by sheep on the land, and is followed by barley, then rape, before turnips again.

Leicester sheep were brought from upcountry in 1790 and bred with our native sheep.

Devon and Shorthorn cattle have partly replaced the black Cornish breed. They are fed on turnips, straw, hay and swedes. Oxen cost more than horses to feed and it takes 4 oxen to do the work of 2 horses. Small Cornish horses graze on rough land and struggle through the winter unhoused and unfed. Stallions of a heavier breed from Wales are not accepted by the little Cornish mares. Working horses must be fed on grass and clover, tares and rye, and in winter oats and chaffed straw and swede, which costs 1/- per horse per day.

The Cornish pig has been crossed with Berkshire and Leicester pigs, and can be fattened on steamed potatoes and barley, otherwise it eats turnips.

Karkeek concluded that while more food was being produced than in 1800 there was still too much waste land.

The work of farm labourers was heavy using wooden and iron ploughs, scarifiers, drills, turnip cutters and horsehoes made and mended by the local blacksmith. The big advance was the thrashing machine of cast iron, powered by running water, by horses or by Richard Trevithick's steam engine. Steam, as a side line, cooked food for farm animals. A skilled man might earn 9/- per week, with a cottage and a plot of his own, or 12/- without. Hamilton Jenkin describes such a man in 1850, who was allowed to keep two pigs for himself and to take wood from the hedges. His working hours were from 6 a.m. to 7 p.m. and his family worked also from 8 a.m. hoeing turnips, weeding corn, picking stones, planting potatoes, rolling barley and oats, haymaking and reaping. Children aged 4 or 5 years earned 4d a day, and the women 6d. According to Hamilton Jenkin they didn't wear shoes and were lightly clothed in all seasons, and children too young or frail to work were left all day in the cottage. Father's jobs were thrashing, carting earth, mixing and carrying manures, ploughing, binding wood, stone and turf hedging, horse-hoeing, thatching and digging drains.

Karkeek describes the uses of a seed/manure drill to sow turnips, from which the harvest should be 25 tons per acre. Cabbages, mangolds and carrots were grown for animal food.

Karkeek goes on to criticise the hay crop in Cornwall. On each acre should be sown 7 gallons of ryegrass, 4 of cocksfoot, 3 lb rough meadow grass, 8 lb red clover. The crop should be cut while green because there is then more sugar in it, and it must be often turned.

He concedes that farmers have not the capital to grow and store any more food, and that carrying lime and manure is expensive. Both human and animal excreta are too much allowed to drain into rivers so ammonia is wasted. He recommends guano and bone meal.

Tenancies should be at least for 21 years and tenants should be free to plan crop rotation. (CN P2 1846)

Karkeek could see room for improvement. But hard times for farmers were coming with the abolition of the Corn Laws and the consequent import of cheap American corn, and then the slump in mining and mass emigration.   Here is a hint of a new trade:
Advertised in *West Briton* 1852: 'Dutch flower roots, hyacinths, tulips,

anemones, ranunculus, narcissus, gladiolus, crocus, snowdrops at Mitchinson's seed store Truro.'

Some remedies offered to farmers in 1839

To cure colds in cattle: take of aniseeds, carraway seeds, grains of paradise and fenugreek, each 2 oz and mix with water. Or sweet fennel seeds, cummin seeds, each 2 oz, long pepper, turmeric, ginger and elecampane each 1 oz in a drink. To administer put in a pitcher with 2 oz butter, 2 tablespoons treacle, add 1 quart boiling ale and cool. 2 hours later give cow a good mash of scalded bran and a handful of ground barley.

Flies on sheep: apply to sore boiled train oil, (squeezed from pilchards) tar and salt.

For horse with worms: Castile soap, chimney soot, crickle button seeds and broil in urine.

New Cattle Plague Orders
A poster from Lostwithiel court in 1867

No animal with plague or in last 28 days in contact shall be placed on unenclosed land. Constable to be notified. Must not be sold, driven along highway or by rail or canal. Not to be removed alive from stable. Local Authority can slaughter and bury and the owner pays if the law is broken. All affected animals to be slaughtered and buried and hide slashed under 6 feet of earth and lime. All dung to be disinfected either by owner or by Local Authority at owner's expense. Cattle may go to market after 28 days and after disinfection. Cattle may not be moved at night; nor to beyond Local Authority.

Imported cattle must have vetinerary certificate and Local Authority licence. Sheep, goats and swine in same ship are subject to same restrictions. Hides to be covered before transport.

Clerk of the Peace Bodmin

(X576122)

Control of Foot and Mouth Act 1869

Rules apply to any stable or shed infected. Animals affected or herded with them not to be moved from field or stable except for slaughter. Sheds to be disinfected to the satisfaction ot the Local Authority.

Signed, Clerk of the Peace, Bodmin.

Bird Turd

Farmers commanded to use more manure had the expense of finding and carrying it. In 1765 it was recorded that for an acre of land to be sown with wheat 20 loads per day of manure were carried for five days, as well as a barge load of sand. The cost of carrying and spreading it was nearly 30/-, the same amount as the profit from the crop. Manure was dung from farm animals, scrapings from the road, and most effective human dung fetched from towns.

There was an easier way. It was William Gibbs of Tyntesfield who promoted it and turned his bankruptcy to a fortune in about 1843, becoming for a while the richest man in England. His discovery was mountains of bird droppings and remains of sea animals, guano, in Peru and around South America. Nesbitt wrote a treatise about the benefits of guano to farmers. There being a shortage of manure in England it was necessary to import some and guano had everything, he said: lime, potassium, sodium to strengthen straw and good for mangelwurzels, phosphate, sulphate good for clover, oxygen, hydrogen and carbon, and above all nitrates.

It needs to be collected dry and free from sand and it is cheaper to carry it from South America than to carry local manure within Cornwall. The best comes from Bolivia and the most from Peru. He compares the nitrogen content of guano with other dung: 1 ton of guano provides as much nitrogen as 33 tons of farm dung, 21 tons of horse dung, 38 tons of cow dung, 22 tons of pig dung, 14 tons of human excrement.

He instructs farmers to mix pulverised guano with wood turf or coal ash on a stone floor and drill it into ground. Apply 2 cwt per acre to wheat in autumn and spring and if wheat droops apply more with 4 cwt of salt. For turnips broadcast 3 cwt before sowing and 1 cwt between drills using horse-hoe. For legumes and flax broadcast before sowing and for potatoes topdress. For grass add 3 cwt per acre in March.

What we owe the Cow.
From a newspaper of 1902

320 sovereigns is the debt we owe to every cow born bred and slaughtered on British soil.

A cow begins giving milk when two years old and a good milch animal should yield in each milk-giving period of 8 - 9 months 5000 gallons of milk from which comes 500 lb of cheese and 200 lb butter worth say £20. The cow is available for milking for 10 years so her milk is worth £200.

She will have 10 calves worth at 6 months old £5 each.

1200 lb live weight animal will give 700 lb dressed beef worth £15. Hide worth 30/-, or tanned and made into boots £40.

Her hair is worth 6d per lb the best being the tail for stuffing sofa and cushions and for barristers' wigs. Short hair makes felt, horsecloths, rugs, roof felt, covering for pipes and boilers.

From interior of horns comes pith for glue, from the hard parts combs and buttons. One pair of horns makes two combs price 2/-. Good horns are like tortoiseshell. The tips make mouthpieces for pipes.

Large bones are for knife handles and toothbrushes. Small bones for buttons and counters.

Waste is fertiliser. Or it can be calcined in a closed retort to become animal charcoal or ivory black paint. A byproduct is alphanaphtha which deters insects.

Hoofs become glue, gelatine and isinglass.

Tallow and grease become soap, worth 40/- per cow, and glycerine for dynamite, vaccine preservative and scent.

Sinews are catgut. Bone marrow is a pomade.

So take care of your cow.

Tools for the Job

Tenants of small farms without oxen or horses had to use their own muscles for ploughing, weeding, sowing, digging, draining, cutting and carrying. In the early part of the century roads were usually muddy tracks, steep and slippery, where carts would stick in the mire or overturn and donkeys were a safer way for carrying loads, escorted by a person on each side to keep the load upright.

A variety of tools were used, made of wood and iron and made and mended at home or by the village carpenter and smith. In 1841 Carnon Downs had 4 carpenters, and a smith with an apprentice; in 1871 there was a wheelwright. Some of the tools can be seen at Helston Folk Museum, at St. Winnow Farm Museum, at Pill Farm on open

Drawing by A.Appleby, copied from *Countryside Remembered* by Sadie Ward days, and they are described in Ray Brigden's *Agricultural Hand Tools* (Shire Publications), and in Sadie Ward's *Countryside Remembered*. Some are drawn here. The forging of tools using the power of waterwheels and fire and hammers still happens at Finch Foundry (National Trust), near Okehampton.

The arrish rake (drawing, page 136) for instance was made entirely of wood. The handle was ash or willow up to 3 metres long, roughly cut, straightened by steam, shaped by knife, and split at one end to be inserted into a board (head pole), in which holes were bored to take tightly fitting wooden teeth.

The scythe of beech wood or willow had a curved wooden handle with pegs of wood as handholds. Attached to it was a loose hazel basket which pushed cut corn out of the way of the next swathe. The handle was as long as a man's height and curved and required a strong skilled man to swing it rhythmically from side to side all day. On a big farm labourers followed one another in strict rhythm and their speed depended on keeping the blade sharp using in the field a sharpened stone or a greased and sanded piece of oak.

Scythes

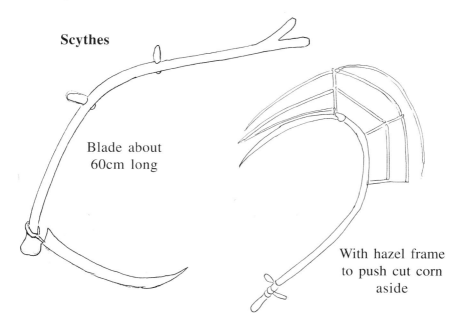

Blade about
60cm long

With hazel frame
to push cut corn
aside

The sickle was light enough to be used by women, and carefully shaped to be worked mainly from the wrist; it worked well when the blade was sharp. A stick in the spare hand was used to gather the cut stalks.

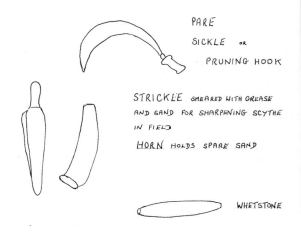

PARE

SICKLE or

PRUNING HOOK

STRICKLE SMEARED WITH GREASE AND SAND FOR SHARPENING SCYTHE IN FIELD

HORN HOLDS SPARE SAND

WHETSTONE

Most of the tools were of iron with wooden handles. There were dung forks and tommyhawkes, tools for prising up docks and stones, dibbers, and cutting tools such as hayknives, bill-hooks, and axes. Clearing waste ground for tilling was bound to be hard and the breast plough was one tool used: a branch was gripped by a sharp triangle of iron at one end, and the other end was split to be inserted into a flat board which a man pushed with chest or thigh, aiming to scrape the top 50 mm off the ground, which had already been burnt. The scrapings were piled and burnt and became part of the manure heap which would have to be spread.

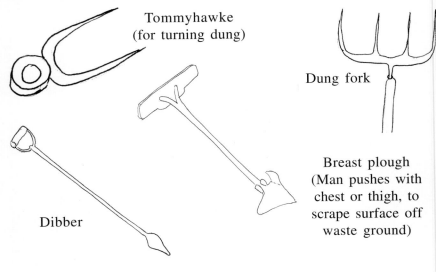

Tommyhawke
(for turning dung)

Dung fork

Dibber

Breast plough
(Man pushes with chest or thigh, to scrape surface off waste ground)

Scattering of seeds had to be done evenly to make the best use of the ground and the seed, and to enable the crop to be weeded. A shallow basket was attached to a man's left side and as he paced the field he flung seed with his right hand each time his right leg moved forward. This required experience especially in windy weather and with light seeds. An advance was the fiddle broadcaster from which seed was released from a box attached to the man, as he moved a bamboo rod like a violinist's bow to and fro crosswise. The mechanism was a finned disc which was turned by the rod and opened and closed the seed box.

Drawing by A.Appleby, copied from *Countryside Remembered* by Sadie Ward

Left: Fiddle broadcaster (Man pulled and pushed straight cane lengthways like playing a fiddle)

No doubt forks and spades were in use as they are now. But there were particular shapes for particular uses. For digging a metre deep V-cross-section drain tapered spades of graded widths were used, and a long narrow scoop on a handle cleared the wet stuff from the bottom. Hoes for weeding were of many shapes, designed for clearing between various crops without treading on them. Hedges, mostly hawthorn, became necessary to separate cattle from crops. and were controlled by bill-hooks and slashers. The aim was to keep the growth dense but not too high or wide. About once in a dozen winters a hawthorn hedge was laid, that is branches were half-cut and bent over and woven in and out of either living stems or driven stakes.

Bill-hooks cut wood and furze on waste land for fuel, for building and for tools, and for making a twiggy base for stacks of hay and straw.

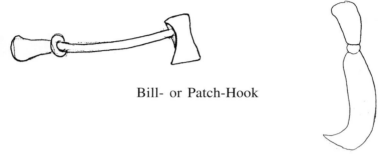

Bill- or Patch-Hook

As seen on the O.S. 1880 large scale map, fields on the east side of the turnpike, at Killiganoon and Tregie, are large with curved and notched boundary hedges, perhaps a relic of pre-Victorian landscape, while on the west side there is a patchwork of small rectangular fields enclosed from waste in the 18th and 19th centuries. The bushes of the hedges are haw and sloe, hazel, holly and occasionally apple, and the sides and tops are clad with grasses, ferns, campions and stitchwort, primroses and violets, sorrel and goosegrass, and three-cornered leek. R.L.Gwatkin of Killiow in about 1800 recommended that for a six foot high hedge a trench six feet wide be dug. Into this was laid a row of large stones, grounders, on each side. Piled into the middle was clay and slate dug from alongside so leaving a ditch, and brought in also from a clay pit. About half the height was to be filled before Christmas and the rest in March, when plant cuttings were inserted, or alternatively turf was laid on top. Meanwhile the sides of the hedge were faced with stones picked from nearby ground, usually quartz because it was abundant in the ground and a hazard to cultivation. The hedge tapers from bottom to top, 'like a lighthouse', with the most taper at the bottom, and the stones were carefully laid so that they stayed in place, wedged sometimes with a finger of couch grass.

Hay-making required the scythe or the sickle, and a hay rake with rounded ashwood teeth. The cut hay was spread in rows to dry and then into round cocks. After a few days' drying pitchforks were needed for carrying the hay to a stack where it was built and thatched. As required for feeding stock hay was cut from the stack with a hefty hay knife with a broad blade some 360 mm long.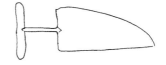

Barley and oats had to be thrashed before 1800 with a flail wielded by hand to separate ears from straw, and then thrown to the wind to separate naked grain from chaff which blew away. Straw was stacked for bedding or chopped by a chaff cutter into pieces up to 20 mm long. Chopped chaff was mixed with chopped turnips for cattle food. Whole turnips were too hard for the teeth of cattle and sheep and the outsides of the roots were wasted.

Home

Of the houses listed in the tithe map some have sunk into the ground, some, like Aylesford, Victoria cottage, The Beeches, 31 Knights Meadow, Chyreen, Upper and Lower Clydia, Chiverton, Trerise, Samaria and Ebenezer, have been made neat and convenient while keeping some 19th century features. It may be that the houses of 1842 have been enlarged, or replaced, and residential parts have become outbuildings or outbuildings have become parts of residences.

Home was where you built it. The big landowners of the 18th and 19th centuries leased a few acres of waste land to a tenant, who was obliged to cultivate it under the landlord's rules, to build or to repair a house on it, to maintain its fertility, while the landlord still had the right to dig for minerals, and to pass through to take water or wood. The lease terminated when the last of three named persons could no longer be proved to be alive, and could be renewed by payment of a fine. Later in the 19th century 21-year leases were more usual. The tenant himself built his home, probably with the help of relatives. Building materials at hand were slate (killas) and clay dug from the site or from the pits and quarries in Bissoe Road, and timber perhaps from waste land. It could be roofed with straw or with scantles (irregular dark grey slates from North Cornwall). Hamilton Jenkin describes such cottages in *Cornwall and its People*.

Having asserted a right of occupation the tenant, between eight-hour cores at the mine, could begin to enclose a few acres for growing hay and potatoes, and to build hedges and sheds to contain his cow and calf, donkey, goat, pig, and cock and hens. In the house the floor was trodden earth; the entrance was through a doorway with an upper and lower door like a stable; a chimney could be added and windows fitted. He needed a wife 'to make butter', that is to fetch water, tip sewage, wash and scrub the houses of themselves and their stock, to dig and weed and cook and mend, as well as to preserve the milk as butter. Boards supported by wooden posts were added at above head height as a sleeping space, and once he had acquired the tools the man might make a chair and a table. The landlord collected rent and tithe.

The house could be of any shape or size and improvements by the tenant increased the value for the landlord, so both benefitted. The basic house had a rectangular front with a door and two many-paned windows at ground level and three windows above. At one end the chimney made a bulge from the ground to the pot on the roof. Founded on large stones the walls were built of cob about 600 mm wide or of killas 450 mm wide bedded in lime mortar. The roof was of timber and laths carrying scantles hung on wood pegs. The alternative roofing, thatch, using straw or water reed bundles tied with willow or hazel was watertight only if the angle of the roof was steep, that is more than 45 degrees from horizontal, and lasted about 25 years if not ruined by rats, sparrows, gales or fire. Some Carnon Downs houses appear to have a ground storey of killas and an upper storey of cob, either or both covered but not water-proofed by lime wash inside and out. The laundry/wash-room/larder/ was a leanto at the back and there was an array of buildings for animals and for storage. At Trerise the wash-house with its fireplace and bowl, and the calf house next to it and the stable and loft are still dry and in good order.

Inside a wide fireplace on the outside wall next to the chimney served to warm the house, for boiling and roasting, and for drying clothes. At one side was a hole in the wall lined with clay which was heated with hot ashes for baking barley bread and cake. 31 Knights Meadow still has such a cloam oven, and there are movable ones in Helston Folk Museum, rounded clay pots with an opening door on one side.

More modern, that is from the later 19th century, was the Cornish range, made in foundries at Redruth and Truro, with the furze (or coal later) fire behind an iron door, an oven beside it with its own door, and hotplates on top. In Feock Parish History Book IV are descriptions of fireplaces and cooking pots and drawings of Cornish ranges at Tresithick House (left, below) and Blacksmith Cottage (right).

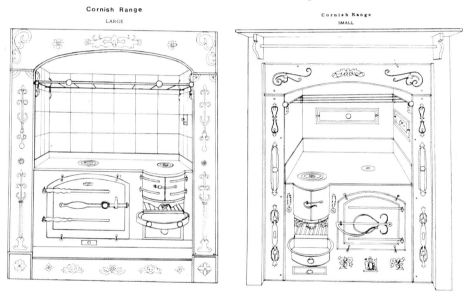

Cornish Range
LARGE

Cornish Range
SMALL

Clay and Straw

Walls of cob last hundreds of years, are strong enough to support the roof, keep out the rain, absorb heat so that they feel cool in summer and warm in winter, emit no poisons, need no factory, and the building of them uses human muscle and skill without harm. While it is kept dry under a good roof and on a stone foundation a cob wall remains hard almost as rock. When unroofed and no longer required the material of the wall can be mixed with water and sand and used again in a new wall, or it can be left slowly to return to the earth whence it came.

Cob is a mix of sand, straw (and manure?) and the clay which underlies Carnon Downs and which in the late 19th century was dug from a pit in part of Lord Falmouth's waste in Bissoe Road. The dry materials are mixed together and with water into a stiff malleable mass. The base of the planned wall is stones, and on to this is piled the sticky cob to a width of about 600 mm, any length and a height of 120 mm. As with pottery it is pressed to squeeze out air bubbles and to keep it mixed. Flat sides are achieved by thwacking and trimming. A thwacker, shown in the sketch, is a wooden cylinder with one flattened side and, holding it by a long wooden handle, the craftsman vigorously beats the sides of the block of wet cob and then with a knife cuts off any projecting bits of straw. The wall is covered with a plastic sheet these days, perhaps 200 years ago with wood or leather, and left for three days before the next 120 mm is built. Corners are finished with 'lime putty' and the surface when dry can be lime washed but must not be waterproofed.

Window and door frames and lintels in 19th century buildings were usually of oak.

In succeeding years extensions, and conversions of outbuildings, have disguised the original houses, and among the modern estates they stand firm and dry.

Early Learning at Home

Not only farmers but nearly every tenant farmed his few acres in order to keep his family. Much depended on their industry and frugality, and the preservation of the harvest from autumn till next summer. It was vital for children not only to learn a trade, for boys mining, sailing, shoemaking, for girls housekeeping and dressmaking, but also from an early age to work on the land.

Milk was not easily obtainable from farms because in the raw state it did not keep well, and it was usual to keep a cow at home. All summer she fed herself on pasture of grass/clover 4:1, and in winter she was indoors and fed on hay, turnips, chopped straw, crushed barley and oilcake. Her calf was born in the spring and was fed skimmed milk from a finger dipped in a bucket. Milk from the cow was left in a bowl overnight for the cream to rise. That bowl was stood in a bigger one of hot water near the fire until the cream became a yellow crust which was skimmed off and eaten or was shaken in a jar until it separated into butter and a watery whey. The butter remained good if kept cool. The calf was either kept to replace the cow or sold, if male, for beef, and the cow herself was sold at up to 10 years old. Such was the demand of domestic animals for skimmed milk that children had little of it.

Hay fields were cut in June while the grass - Timothy, Foxtail, Coxfoot, Fescues - was flowering but still juicy, friends and neighbours helping. It was spread to dry, mixed sometimes with clover, lucerne and sainfoin, and in the evening raked into windrows or small cocks. After as many days as it took to dry it was carried and thrown on to a base of twigs and bracken, piled and pressed and trodden, and thatched. During the winter a portion of hay was cut out as required with a hay knife, a heavy blade with handles for two hands.

In the 1920 sales lists of Lord Falmouth and of Captain Tremayne there are houses with stalls for cows. A shed about 4 x 2 metres, built of cob or stone and roofed with tiles, with a floor of stone slabs laid on earth, could house 3 cows, each one with her own space partitioned from the others. A rope round the cow's neck was attached by a chain to a stittle, that is an iron pole on which a link of chain could slide up and down. In front of the cow was a stone bowl fixed into the wall at head level and containing hay to which she could help herself. Behind her and near the door was a gulley into which wet dirt drained on its way to the dung heap.

STITTLE

Milking was done in the same shed, the cow tied and munching. The farmer, or his wife or child, sat on a stool on one side of the cow leaning the side of his head into her flank. The bucket stood on the floor under the cow, who, being restless because of biting flies, might kick it over or whip her tail in the farmer's face. Whether the cow let down her milk easily depended on her familiarity with the farmer and his firm grasp on two of her teats with his hands. Any spilt milk was licked by the family cat who might also lap from the bucket if allowed. During the summer a bull keeper led his bull through the lanes and was paid to supervise the impregnation of cows as required.

Roads were not the obstacle that they are now. People who were children in the 1940s and living in Old Carnon Hill, remember Miss Julian driving her herd of cattle daily across the road from Trerise to the fields of Smithy Lane and home again, reminiscent of previous centuries when roads were for meeting people on their domestic errands.

Training on the Job

While a miner in the 19th century might with luck earn £2 in a month, a skilled agricultural labourer might earn 36/- per month with a cottage and perhaps a potato patch and a patch for pigs included. For the beginner the wage was less.

There were 12 agricultural labourers in Carnon Downs in 1841 and more in 1871, when there were 12 farmers who might have employed them. Hamilton Jenkin describes the family of a farm worker: The working hours were from 6 a.m. to 7 p.m. for the father. The women and children, having completed the chores in their home, set out to work in the fields at 8 a.m. and there remained until 6 p.m. Their work was weeding the corn, hoeing turnips, picking out stones, rolling barley and oats, reaping with a sickle, raking and carrying hay. The women were paid 6d a day and the children from the age of four years 3d. It meant that the children learnt early to work on the land, and their little wage was essential to the family, so that the attendance officer for Devoran school in the 1870s had to report the absence of children who were busy picking potatoes and stones. For those children a government grant could not be claimed and the school was therefore the poorer.

Boys and girls from the age of 12 years, and also parish apprentices, were employed on farms and accommodated. The first meal of the day, says Hamilton Jenkin, was 'sky blue and sinker' made of water, barley flour, and scald milk, boiled and served with a lump of barley bread at the bottom. Reverend Hawker of Morwenstow describes sweet, tasty, crusty, barley bread, oaten cakes, and huge pies, 'a hillock of brown dough and steaming puffs' containing anything available, often conger eels, pilchards and oysters, butter and cream, or hiding young rooks, mutton, veal or bacon, with apple, pepper and salt.

> 'Scads 'n tates, scads 'n tates,
> Scads 'n tates 'n conger,
> And those who can't eat scads 'n tates
> O they must die of hunger.'

It was the farmer's wife who had to provide for her family and the labourers, earning what she could by selling bacon, poultry, cheese, butter, cream and honey to the wives of miners and other workers. In the fire place she had a kettle hanging over a brandis, and a spit which had to be turned, and a baking kettle which was a pot inverted over hot ash. Crocks were made of clay or brass. The fire had to be lit by striking flint on iron over tinder, which was a cotton rag soaked in saltpetre and dried. Fuel was furze and logs. A quick flame could be obtained by dipping a slither of wood in melted brimstone and touching the lighted tinder with it. Matches were not used until about 1890.

The Problem with Turnips

Turnips as a first crop on newly cleared land, and sheep let loose on the crop to eat it and to drop manure, was the method recommended for converting barren land to arable. But turnips need weeding and because they were irregularly sown weeding was a job done on hands and knees, and slow. The solution to weeding turnips was invented by Jethro Tull in 1702 but not adopted in Cornwall for maybe more than a century, perhaps because it was designed to be pulled by horses. Tull's turnip drill was three boxes carried on four wheels. Seeds from the boxes fell through tubes which cut holes in the ground so that the seeds were buried. A

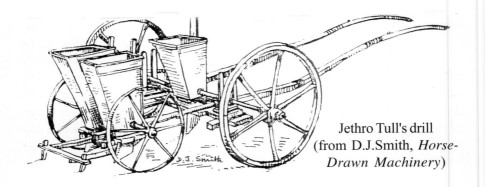

Jethro Tull's drill
(from D.J.Smith, *Horse-
Drawn Machinery*)

horse between shafts pulled the drill, guided by a man to keep him in straight lines. The result was even rows of turnips, and weeding could be done with a hoe, likewise pulled by a horse. Later drills injected manure at the same time as seed.

IF YOU HAD A HORSE

Tenants farming two or three acres as most did in Carnon Downs continued to clear their ground, plough, sow, weed, and harvest with only hand tools. But on bigger farms like Higher Devoran, Killiganoon and Tregye, horses pulled a variety of ingenious machines. Some can be seen at Pill Farm, some abandoned in fields. For a clear and technical account with detailed drawings read D.J. Smith's *Discovering Horse-drawn Machinery* (Shire Publications, 1979), from which I can only pass on a few extracts. Sadie Ward's *Countryside Remembered* (Cameron Books) contains photographs and memories of farm work in England in the first half of the 20th century. In the Cornwall Records Office there are catalogues of machines on show and for sale in the 19th century.

Farmers having bought or borrowed a horse made some tools of their own, for instance a wooden rack bearing gorse branches to rake soil, and a newly painted board to be dragged across turnips to trap the turnip fly. If you could afford it, in the 19th century there were ever more efficient machines for ploughing, clod breaking, cultivating, harrowing, rolling, drilling, reaping, cutting hay, raking, carrying corn, and the biggest operation of all, thrashing.

Ploughs

The object was to turn a few inches of soil to the side leaving a furrow. Before 1800 some ploughs were entirely of wood. An iron ploughshare was later added to the wooden board which turned the turf and was kept sharp. Knives, coulters, cut through turf in advance of the share. Ransomes in E. Anglia hardened the iron parts and made them self-sharpening. The essential parts of the plough were: a chain at the front to be attached to a horse's traces, two wheels of different diameters to fit into the top and bottom of the furrow, a pair of coulters, a curved board fitted with a sharp iron share, and a pair of long handles at the back with which the farmer guided the plough.

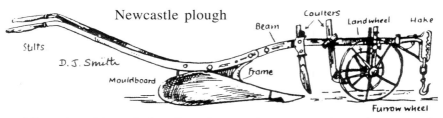

Newcastle plough

After ploughing clods of earth were beaten to pieces by mattocks, unless one of many varieties of cultivator was available. The aim was to drag over the ground rows of curved sharp tines mounted under a frame on wheels. In some designs the tines could be raised and lowered, and in some the tines were rigid and in others sprung. In some the farmer was seated instead of walking and in some one wheel could be lowered, or the tines could be adjusted for hoeing.

Alternatively or in addition to using a cultivator, there were drags and rollers. A drag was a square of planks nailed together overlapping and pulled over the ground. A roller could be simply a tree trunk. Others were made from stone, wood, iron or latterly concrete. Granite rollers are to be found still in use as gate posts or in stiles. The solid roller was free to rotate on its frame while the horse pulled.

Harrows were horse-drawn rakes, an elaboration of drags. Some were like a sledge with spikes underneath. The spikes could be curved or splayed, blunt or sharp. More elaborate were the zig-zag and the chain harrows in which multiple metal spiky rods, or pieces of chain, were linked together, sometimes conforming to the contours of the land by springs. These were used to prepare a seedbed and to cover seeds after sowing.

Sowing and hoeing

Weeding was the work of women and children, and was easier when seeds were mechanically drilled in straight rows, which also made it possible to hoe with a horse-hoe. The horse pulled a triangular frame, under which were the legs of hoes with their feet arrowshaped, point forward. The farmer walked behind to control the path of the machine so as not to damage the plants, and a horse I am told carefully walked between rows. The blades, or feet, had to be at the right distance apart for each crop.

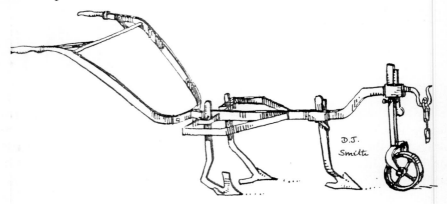

Iron-framed one-row hoe
(from D.J.Smith, *Horse-Drawn Machinery*)

This is why Jethro Tull's drill was the important advance in machinery. Concentrating on avoiding the dreary labour of weeding by hand he studied horse-hoes and made their use possible by inventing a seed drill which made holes for the seeds, dropped the seeds into the holes, and covered the seeds with earth. His machine could sow 3 tons of seed in one session, writes D.J. Smith. Later modifications squirted manure at the same time. Tull's invention was in 1701 but was hardly used for another 100 years, for the reason that it put farm labourers out of work, and also that tenants feared that improvements in soil condition would increase the value of the land and therefore their rents.

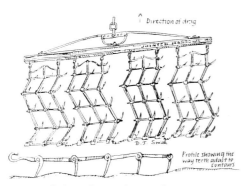

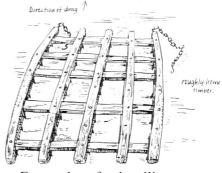

Jointed or zigzag harrow   Frame drag for levelling

Drawings by D.J.Smith

Hay and Corn

The harvest was helped by increasingly efficient machines. One of the first was a horsedrawn mower which carried a long bar and blade protruding at one side at a right angle. The corners of the field were opened up with a scythe leaving the rest of the field clear for the horse to pull the mower in a circular course. Other machines raked and turned the cut grass and even the building of a haystack was helped by a horse lifting bundles of hay by walking to and fro with a rope through an elevated pulley. For cutting corn there was first a

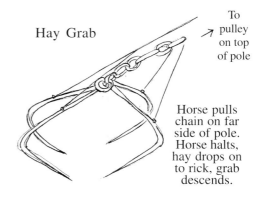

Hay Grab

To pulley on top of pole

Horse pulls chain on far side of pole. Horse halts, hay drops on to rick, grab descends.

reaper, and then a reaper-binder which bundled the corn into sheaves ready for men to tie them. The big advance was the thrashing machine.

The bound sheaves were built at once into an arrish-mow, that is one upright sheaf with one on each side leaning on it, two more in the gaps, four more outside those, and some more on top to deflect rain. When dry enough the sheaves were moved to the rickyard or mowhay by horse and cart. The floor of the rick was boards a metre above the ground and

131

standing on granite 'toadstools' to prevent rats from burrowing in the straw. The rick was thatched with straw or rushes, and the farmer's wife entertained the labourers with boiled beef and chicken, and plum puddings

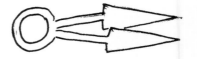

Sheep or thatching shears

and cream and buns, cider and beer. There were songs and games and shouting, and at last a quiet stroll home in the moonlight.

Drawing by
A.Appleby based on
Sadie Ward's photo

During the winter the rick had to be taken apart and the sheaves separated into straw, husks and grain. Without machinery this was done by flailing the beards to dislodge the grains, or by rolling them with granite rollers on hard ground. The straw was removed and chopped and the grains and husks were shaken in a basket so that the wind blew away the husky bits (doust) leaving a basket full of grain. This was thrashing and winnowing, and there were machines to do it since the beginning of the 19th century, either fixed or pulled from farm to farm by horses, who also powered the machinery. Sheaves of corn were untied and fed in, ears first, straw was rubbed, tossed and discarded, and both grain and awns fell into sacks. Heavier machines winnowed as well, delivering grain ready for the mill. It was hard for the horses and Richard Trevithick persuaded Christopher Hawkins of Trewithen to use a steam engine with power equivalent to four horses and for about one eighth the cost, and needing only two labourers. It could be used for every heavy job on the farm, Trevithick said, and could be pulled through fields and lanes by horses and could be lent to other farms. Coal was cheap.

Drawing by A.Appleby based on
Sadie Ward's photo

By the 1950s thrashing machines were hired by the big farms eg Higher Devoran from John Wearne at the garage, John Bassett at Three-mile-stone, Carlyon at Baldhu, or Little Beside at St Day. Little had changed in the last century. The farmer, after milking and putting the cattle out, had to have ready enough coal to feed the machine and take it to the next farm, and a tankful of water from a river, several balls of binder twine, clean barns, and croust of scones, heavy cake and white cake with gallon jugs for milky tea. At 6.00 a.m. some of the thrashing team lit the fire in the greased and oiled engine and were given breakfast of potatoes, fried bread and egg, sausages and bacon.

The thrashing machine was installed on the mowhay among the ricks. Ten men were needed to do the work: two to pass sheaves from the rick to the thrashing set, one to cut the strings from the sheaves, one to feed the loose sheaves into the thrasher, three on top of the machine, two building the straw into a new rick, one loading a cart with sacks of grain to be pulled by a horse to a barn. Jugs of tea were provided all day and croust came at 10 a.m. and 3.30 p.m.

At the end of the day the thrashing set, that is the steam engine and trucks full of equipment, and the living accommodation for the men, trundled along the lanes to the next farm.

Horses were still doing heavy work on farms until the 1950s. Charlie at Middle Devoran was an ex-cavalry horse with small hooves, who drew a hoe without stepping on the plants and turned round without supervision at the ends of rows. He also pulled a hay-pole which hooked hay from wagon to rick. There were 2 pairs of shire horses at Higher Devoran, who pulled the reaper-binder after the corners of a field had been scythed by hand. Cart wheels were made at the carpenter's shop next to Kiddleywink and the iron binds were put on by Webber and Jennings, who also made and sharpened tines for harrows.

Drawing by A.Appleby based on Sadie Ward's photo

If you had a donkey you could carry two sacks of barley on its back, or you could ride to market in a shay (a plank on two wheels). A mule (the sterile product of crossing a donkey with a mare) was stronger and was employed in packs of hundreds by the mines, each one able to carry 2 sacks of ore along steep stony lanes and through mire.

The Cornish breed of horse was the Goonhilly, small and surefooted, which 'struggled through the winter unhoused and unfed', that is it was left in the fields (C.R.O.CN/P/2). This report recommended that for 1/- per horse per day it should be fed in winter on steamed chaffed straw, turnips and potatoes, and oats. A strong obedient horse could be put to work carrying hay on its back, or walking in circles turning a horse whim. J.N. Thomas (C.R.O. 265/11) described the nineteenth century farmer and his wife going to market, each sitting on two sacks of corn on a horse, and the wife carrying her basket. From Higher Devoran the route was along B.R. 24 to the main road.

If you didn't grind your barley at home it could be carried to a mill, of which there were two on the Quenchwell Road marked on the 1880 map. One was opposite the lane to Chyreen and the other a field's width further north. Miss Philbrick and Miss Bowring at Algarnick Cottage remember the base of the latter on their plot, and said it was burnt down in about 1918. The nearest running water was the source of the stream in Valley Lane, and at the road level hardly enough to drive a mill, so perhaps it was steam powered. The miller charged about 1/12 the price of the corn. Mills with water conducted through leats were Edwards' at Perranarworthal, and Hicks and Point mills at Bissoe.

Carts before 1800 were not practical because of the potholes and floods as described by both Celia Fiennes and Carew, and travel required a horse with courage and steady feet. After the investment in toll roads and the better surfacing of lanes with broken stones you might harness your horse to a trap, a cart with a side door, carrying three passengers facing forward and decorated with lamps and an umbrella; or to a jingle, with a back door and passengers facing to the back and sides.

News from the *West Briton*

1811 'To be sold in Redruth 20 very capital young mules and horses with saddles and sacks.'

1812 '... admirably suited for manure ... town dung may be procured ... at 1/- per butt load.'

1816 'W.H. and H.P. were indicted for stealing flower roots ... the only one to which the prosecutor would swear was an American shrub called rhododendron ... sentenced to 6 months hard labour and to be publicly whipped through Truro.'

1822 '... occupiers of land in Cornwall, labouring under distress from the unprecedented low price of agricultural produce, oppressed by taxation, rent, rates, tithes, request a meeting (with the high sheriff) to consider relief.'

1823 '... objectionable smoky taste our butter acquires from the milk being scalded over a furze or turf fire ... churning would save fuel.'

1823 'We recommend to our agricultural friends the utility of salt in improving hay, used when ricks are constructed. The late removal of the heavy duty on salt has rendered it available. Cattle eat salted hay with avidity.'

1837 'At Bosvigo farm 150 rats were killed in 3 hours by a Newfoundland and a terrier.'

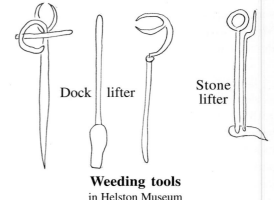

Dock | lifter

Stone lifter

1839 'April is a good time to sow furze seed in clay soils' (yields provender for horses, cattle and sheep, explains R. M. Barton).

Weeding tools
in Helston Museum

1840 'After a shower wireworms may be picked up by children and their ravages prevented.'

1845 'Barque Alchymist from Ichaboe with 200 tons of guano. Apply to Foxes and Co. Perran Wharf.'

Arrish rake
2 metres wide
Handle 2.4 metres long

1847 Meeting of Agriculture Society of Cornwall. 'Canon Philpotts spoke in warm terms of the active benevolence exerted in the parish by Mr Gilbert and other landowners in the prevention of distress. He mentioned the order given by landowners last winter that work was to be given to any man who sought it ... no limit of any kind, and when the smelting works in the parish stopped and 120 men were thrown out of employ at an hour's notice, not one man was thrown on the poor rate, not one man lost a week's work who wished to work.'

1847 'Cornwall Agriculture report on subsoil ploughing and use of seaweed at Trelissick.'

1852 'Hussey's reaping machine ... the entire width is 8 feet.'

1874 'Great demand for donkeys up the country.'

Making the seat of a chair

A . A

Drawing by A.Appleby, copied from *Countryside Remembered* by Sadie Ward

Middle Devoran 1930

Ebenezer: "One man and his dog"
Cabbages to be sold at the village market

THE STAMP OF WORKING BOOTS

The engine houses of
Unity Wood mine at
Wheal Bush

In the area from Treliever in the west to Come-to-good in the east and
from the Kea boundary in the north to the Carnon River there were in
1841 some 112 households containing 600 people. In 1871 the same
number of people lived in 136 houses, and after that there were fewer
people because of mining and agricultural slump and consequent
emigration especially of young men.

Households were crowded in 1841, but there was more arable land
than now and the possibility of growing crops, keeping livestock and
practising a trade at home. Big farms employed labourers and servants,
roads needed repair, and within walking distance there were the industries
of mining, smelting, and transport whether by mule, horse or donkey or
at Devoran dock or on the Redruth & Chasewater railway.

In Carnon Downs in 1841 130 men and 21 women described
themselves as employed, meaning I suppose that they were paid to work,
while the rest, mainly women, carried water, dug and weeded, cooked
and washed and sewed, and brought up pigs, cows, chicken and children.

Occupations listed	Number of employees in Carnon Downs
Miners	24
Tin miners	12
Copper miners	4
Arsenic miners	2
Farmers	11
Agricultural labourers male and female	14
General labourers	9
Porters (Devoran Dock?)	10
Servants 15 male and 6 female	21
Shoemakers	5
Carpenters	4
Carriers	3
Dressmakers (female)	3
Grocers	3
Seamen	3
Limeburner, coalmeter, innkeeper (Emma Nichols), shipwright, shipwright apprentice, agent on wharf, blacksmith, nurse, pattern-maker, railway agent, tinsmith, gardener, clergy, blacksmith apprentice	1 each
Coal porter, waggon driver, butcher, agent, mason, lead smelter, pilot, waterman	2 each

It is noticeable that no-one worked in Truro, and most of the jobs were both skilled and physical, and some required a walk of several miles there and back. By 1871 there were fewer miners and more working on farms and as housekeepers.

Near at hand was the Carnon Valley filled 20 feet deep with ochreous mud washed down from the Gwennap mines, especially since the County Adit poured into the river at Twelveheads. 'A desert of red sand heaped into vast piles ... while here and there in the trenches might be seen tinners working knee deep in water and a few squalid half-clad boys wheeling the tin ore to the stream head in barrows.' (George Henwood ?1853)

Webber and Jennings at the blacksmith's shop

The right to dig in the mud for tin was granted from landowners to adventurers like John Williams who then apportioned patches to working miners: 'John Williams of Carnanton grants to John Williams of Gwennap a sett for 21 years to stream tin on the north side of the Carnon River between turnpike gate and Bissoe Bridge, reserving to the lessor the counting house with stable on north side and courtledge on the west.' (DDWH 5476 year 1803)

'Surviving executor of Samuel Enys and guardian of his son John grant to Thomas and Richard Michell of Gwennap tinners to work and search for tin in all of the 4/9 of a moiety of and in all that ground now covered with mud and slime being part of Carnon Crease as far south as their right extends ... and up and down the valley for 21 years. Thomas and Richard are to pay to the guardians 4/9 of a moiety of 1/14 part at the smelting house of all tin and tin stuff that shall be broke ... and will work in the said premises in the most effectual manner with as many men as the workings can conveniently take ... unless hindered by extremity of water and shall ... give 2 days notice to guardians of every division to be made of the tinstuff. If they default or if they leave the work for 6 months unwrought then the sett shall be yielded up and void.' (EN 152.5 year 1784)

Industrial Employment 1800-1900

From 1841 to 1861 the number of miners dropped and of railway workers, watermen, farmers and agricultural labourers increased. More women were employed, and some children, from 3 years old, went to school.

| 1800 | 1810 | 1820 | 1830 | 1840 | 1850 | 1860 | 1870 | 1880 | 1890 | 1900 |

Consols and United Mines   Clifford United

John Williams   John Taylor   John Taylor
opens United   opens Consols sells Consols
                 employs 3000   gear

Killifreth

Wheal Unity Wood

Poldice

Old Wheal Jane

Wheal Baddern Baldhu

Bissoe Arsenic works

Wheal Jane/Nangiles mundic   closed 1908

Bissoe Works: vitriol, Conn and Todd arsenic, copper precipitation, tin smelting

Bassett foundry   bone works

                                    Visick's
                                    engineering

Perran Wharf

Perran Foundry   employed 600

Carnon Mine   Carnon Yard   Restronguet Creek Tin

Penpol Lead Smelter   Penpol Tin Smelter

Kennal Vale Gunpowder

Redruth-Chasewater Railway   closed 1918

                          Copper slump   Tin slump

Salt tax   Cornwall Railway to Falmouth

Corn Riots
       Corn Laws restricted imports. American corn imported
                repealed 1849
                          Agriculture slump
                          Food riots
                          Emigration

The Michells were tributers, that is, they undertook to dig for tin on a sett and to give up to the leaseholder or owner an agreed fraction of the product which would have to be brought to grass, that is, above ground, and displayed and divided.

The Carnon river down to Point was the subject of a similar contract: 'John Tillie Coryton of Pentillie Castle grants to James Mitchell of St Austell miner ... liberty to dig work mine and search for tin and all other ores from Higher Carnon Bridge to Daniell's Point and erect and build any engines mills and sheds and sink shafts and carry away metals doing as litle damage as possible and not interfering with any other sett ... for next 21 years delivering to John Coryton on the grass at the mine or at stamps or smelting house one full 20th part of all such ores being first spalled and made merchantable and smelted at cost of James Michell and James Michell shall work all lodes unless hindered by want of water and shall pay rates and taxes and keep accounts and John Coryton may inspect same. James Michell will build a good fire engine and John Coryton may go to the bottom of the said mine to examine and may use any ropes buckets windlass kibbles and ladders for any purpose and may work any lode for his own use. The mine is to be kept in perfect repair and clear of rubbish and not allowed to be choaked'. (CY3804 year 1824)

Carnon Stream Works

'A great natural obstacle was to be overcome - ten feet of tidal water and an overburthen of 15 - 30 feet of sand, debris and alluvial deposit.'

To keep out the tide embankments and a dam were built at Tallacks Creek, but were swept away by a storm in 1812. Until then 'the tinners were as undisturbed in their vocations as if no tidal water existed ... small percolations were disposed of by a steam engine.' Sir William Lemon had backed that scheme and backed the 1824 one also:
'Unwilling as I am to have the river again defaced and my comforts at Carclew broken upon by tinners going over all my grounds, and that for what I am convinced will not answer to the adventurer, yet, when everyone is endeavouring to find out labour for the poor ... I must not bear the odium of discouraging mining in Cornwall.'

So in 1824 the engine house, now called Carnon Mine, east of Tallack's Creek, was built and pumped water from a shaft 50 feet under mud, lasted 4 years and made a profit of £28,000.

There were two later ventures to mine under Restronguet Creek, at Carnon Yard from 1835 to 1842, and at Point from 1871 to 1874. Carnon Downs miners in 1842 would have had to take setts in the Carnon river at their own expense or to travel to work in the great mines of Gwennap, Redruth and Chacewater.

Gwennap mines, that is Consolidated and United, with shafts and engine houses from Twelveheads to Carharrack, closed in 1805, unable to make a profit from copper. They were described in 1787 by William Beckford: 'One stumbles on ladders that lead into utter darkness or funnels that exhale cuprous vapours. All around these openings the ore is piled up in heaps ready for purchasers. I saw it drawn reeking out of the mine by the help of a whim put in motion by mules which in their turn are stimulated by impish children hanging over the poor brutes flogging them without respite. The dismal scene of whims, suffering mules and hillocks of cinders extends for miles. Huge iron engines creaking and groaning invented by Watt and tall chimneys smoking and flaming ... and woeful figures in tattered garments with pick axes on their shoulders ... crawled out of a dark fissure and repaired to a hovel which I learnt was a ginshop.'

Cargoes of Tin, and a Pot of Butter

Based on family letters and accounts, an article with this title was contributed to Old Cornwall Society archives by P.N. Tregoning. He lists the ships in which his forebears invested money, and their voyages. His article provides a picture of thriving industries at Bissoe, Kennal Vale and Devoran.

Three partners, William Tregoning, Richard Sampson and Henry Williams, between them invested in 20 ships, some, for instance the 'William Henry', built at Yard, others built at Padstow, Fowey, Llanelli and Appledore. Their business interests were wide.

R.M. Sampson (died 1872) of Park View, Devoran, now Killigarth, was a merchant and agent, had a wharf at Devoran, and managed Bissoe smelter and Kennal Vale Powder works. He caused unease in Devoran by storing gunpowder on the quay; maybe it was he who proposed a gunpowder store near Wellington Place.

William Henry Tregoning (1816 - 1875) was his senior partner at Bissoe and a copper buyer and invested in land, mines and railway companies. His brother John Simmons Tregoning (d. 1878) worked in Liverpool, leaving his son 'Little John' (1842 -1909) with grandmother at West Trevarth, Lanner, from where he rode frequently to Bissoe on a pony. When Little John was 12 William Henry wrote to John Simmons: 'I send to you by this post a letter addressed to you by Little John who is quite well and happy. He is here at Bissoe again today and I purpose taking him to Restronguet to see our new ship this evening.'

So the two of them rode along the shore of the Carnon river and Restronguet Creek, or perhaps along the railway, to Penpol.

Smelted tin from Bissoe was sent as part cargo to tinplate works at Llanelli. Another regular voyage was in the sloop 'Kate' sailed between Truro and Falmouth by William Trebilcock and Charles Gay. Longer trips were to Swansea, Spain, the Baltic and the West Indies with a crew of 5 or 6. The Welsh trip took 16 days and the West Indies 6 months. A mate's wage was £5 per month and a boy earned £1.10. Rations on board were 'sufficient without waste'. Each man had a daily pound of bread, with his ration of beef, pork, flour, peas, tea, coffee, butter, sugar and water.

The 'William Henry' had a more informal errand, the delivery of a present. William Henry wrote to Little John in 1867 asking if he would like some more Cornish butter in his earthenware pot, to which John replied, 'I am much obliged to you by the kind allusion to the butter pot. I believe its contents were not consumed until about 10 days ago and the present has proved a very valuable one. Sophie was only too glad of your kind offer to refill it, and at once sent the pot down to Captain Owens of the 'William Henry' who will deliver it to John Trythall for transmission to West Trevarth.'

Trythall was the technical man in charge of production at Bissoe smelter. It seems that Captain Owens was to refill the pot with butter, and send it to Bissoe. Trythall could hand it to a brakesman on the up train to Redruth, who could deliver it to West Trevarth garden as the train passed by on the south slope of Carn Marth.

Boom and Bust and Boom and Bust

As mine shafts were sunk deeper in the 18th century they were drained by windlass and bucket worked by horse whim or by water wheels, and rag and chain pumps worked by men turning handles. Borlase said, 'Inhabitants have their attention so much engrossed by tin and copper that agriculture and other employments are neglected in the greedy quest for metals'. Tin was profitable and copper, previously discarded, overtook it in value. Consolidated Mines employed over 1000 copper miners (Jenkin p 91). During the latter half of the century John Williams of Scorrier, manager of William Lemon's Poldice, drove the Great Adit from Twelveheads for 30 or 40 miles to drain 46 mines up to 6 miles away, including the mines of Gwennap (Lemon's), Chacewater (Falmouth's) and Camborne-Redruth (Basset's). Deeper lodes of copper were discovered and to pump water up to the adit level 'fire engines' were installed, that is boilers heated by coal and their steam driving pistons. Wheal Busy had a Boulton and Watt engine in 1778. The miners still had to climb down ladders or risk swinging in a bucket on a rope. For the mine lords the middle of the century boomed and yet by 1790 copper mining nearly finished.

The slump was the result of precarious foreign markets, and of the smelters who offered less for ore when it was hard to sell, and of the discovery of a mass of copper ore near the surface of a mountain on Anglesey. Within a decade Anglesey copper was exhausted and the price rose, but by then some of the mines were losing money and were idle: Consolidated, United, Chacewater and Poldice, Dolcoath, Tresavean, mines which had employed thousands of men and boys. In all Cornwall 16,000 were employed in mining in 1801. Because some copper mines turned to tin it was overproduced and the price fell. Boulton and Watt, who had made possible the increased production in the 18th century, continued to take their dues and reasoned that if they did not it would help the mining lords briefly but would not help the market. Boulton, a humane character, hoped the miners would turn their hands to other employ and would be reconciled to their fate (Hamilton Jenkin p 159) The miners sought work in tin so that there was too much of that too. At the same time earthenware crockery was fashionable instead of pewter plates so the demand for tin and lead was reduced. There was also the war with France which disrupted foreign trade. Desperate starving miners rioted, demanding cheaper corn, and blaming smelters and Boulton and Watt for their loss of work and low wages. Watt feared something like the French Revolution, and Boulton wished he could mitigate the distress but observed that mines cannot continue at a loss, and also that he would not 'send Flower from London ... lest they should talk of Arsenic'. (Was he saying that the miners were rioting about poisoned flour?)

Mine lords distributed their own money to the destitute and supplied barley and fish. Lord de Dunstanville's brother-in-law swore in 80 constables who took 80 rioters from their beds at 2 a.m. and one was hanged as an example. Boulton proposed sending miners to lead and coal mines in other counties. What saved the mines by the start of the 19th century was a new market in China and a gradual drop in costs and rise in metal prices. The next boom began.

The first half of the nineteenth century was a good time for Carnon Downs. The population increased, the chapel and houses were built, children learned to read in Sunday school, and at last consideration was given to the health of miners.

The mud at Bissoe Bridge produced 44 tons of black tin from 1833 to 1839 (Dines survey). Consols in Gwennap, abandoned in 1805, was reopened by John Taylor in 1818 and became the biggest copper producer in the country with 63 miles of underground workings. He was keen to renew his lease in 1839 but was not allowed. He therefore sold everything in it that was movable, including tons of copper ore, and the output under new management was halved. United Mines were increasingly productive and by 1857 18 engines had brought up 1,000,000 tons of copper from United plus Consols plus Clifford. So Carnon Downs miners had a chance to work there if they could walk the distance.

Some of the other mines had converted from copper to tin mining and had survived the slump at the end of the 18th century. Around Chacewater Killifreth, Unity Wood and Unity were producing copper, tin, arsenic and lead. Poldice, Creegbrawse and Wheal Maid were still producing copper, tin, arsenic, zinc and ochre. Even Wheal Henry, on the hill between Poldice and the upper Twelveheads to Chacewater road, was still producing copper.

The group of mines Nangiles and the Wheal Janes may have been worked for tin for three centuries. Penaluna described 'extensive caverns quite open to the surface' in the years before fire engines. Sulphuric acid from Nangiles 'would rot a pair of boots off a man's feet in a day'. West Wheal Jane, 'Black Mine', the one that was reopened in 1968, employed 200 people from 1860 -70, and the other Wheal Jane at Goodern worked for a little longer, and Baddern only briefly for lead.

Further afield on the Great Flat Lode around Pool and Carn Brea Basset and Buller mines were producing tin and copper, and to the north there were copper, tin and lead mines around St. Agnes. So there was work for those who were strong enough.

Tut and Tribute

There were two ways of employing miners, both of them having to be bargained beforehand.

One was to lease from a landowner a likely plot and mark it with stones at each corner. For instance Michael and Alexander Allen of Saveock argued insistently for their 200-year-old family right to dig for tin in Baldhu, including Sperries, Hugus, Penweathers, Chacewater, Creag Brawse, Cocks, Todpool and Gew, and to take a fraction of the ore. This was 'bounding' and a variation was 'tributing'.

A tributer agrees with a mine captain at the counthouse to dig what ore he can at his own expense and to take for himself a certain percentage of it. The mine owner would be responsible for the pumps and engines and may inspect, while the tributer must put in timber, keep the mine safe, and return all tackle in good condition. The team working with him was a 'pare'. At Carn Barges in St Agnes miners were to drive 70 fathoms east on any lode they may discover and to keep the mine working, for which they must pay the owner 1/12 of all tin they bring to the smelting house. For white tin, that is smelted tin, the owner usually took 1/12 and for stone at grass, that is unsmelted, 1/9. The ore was measured in barrows and distributed on a field for the owner to fetch his due. That was the case for tin. Copper ore was sold and the money divided according to a bargain written at the counthouse. For a poor lode a tributer would agree to take a larger fraction of the value, and for a rich lode a smaller. He provided his own gunpowder, candles, tools, repairs, and a team of women and children on the surface to break the ore, and hoped to make about £1 per week. Sometimes he made much more, sometimes less, according to the richness of his allotted ground.

Tutworkers undertook to sink a shaft or to drive a crosscut at an agreed sum per fathom. Miners competed among themselves for the work by offering to accept less pay for the same work, a system which kept their wages down. If the ground was hard it took longer to earn their pay, which was about £2 per month. Other work, such as building an engine house or chimney, digging leats, making roads and sawing, were on contract also.

Wages of skilled men in 1841 were about 2/6 per day and of labourers 1/9. (Robert Blee, Royal Cornwall Polytechnic Society 1871)

Some prices were:

Flour ½ peck	3/6	Salt, pepper	8½d
Tea lb	6/-	Candles for a week	4d
Sugar lb	8d	Rent for a week	1/6
Currants lb	10d	Fuel for a week	1/4
Soap lb	6d	Club money, clothes	1/5
Starch	6½d	Lying-in fee	?
Treacle 2 lb	2½d		
Fish 3 lb	6d		
Pork lb	7d		

Some miners received no wages until they had worked two months because a month's wage was kept back to pay for tools. Often they were paid in kind, or compelled to shop at the mine store. Without the cash they could not buy food while at work. There were deductions from wages for the mine doctor and barber; R.M. Barton states that miners could pay 3d per month to be shaved at the mine. The mine lords bore the expenses which the miners could not afford, for a surgeon to attend after an accident, for carrying a hurt man home, a guinea a month to a miner laid up by a mining accident, and funeral expenses.

Families lived mainly on fish and barley and potatoes in season; those with a few acres of land might keep a pig or goat or chickens.

On average tributers earned more than tutworkers but they took a gamble: some struck lucky while others made a loss. The calculation of their pay was punitive: in a case quoted by Hamilton Jenkin two men brought to grass ore worth £13.11s, from which at 13/4 in the £ they were entitled to £9.0.8d. This is high mathematics for a start. Then came deductions:

Subsist (that is, a loan to be repaid)
Materials, smith, drawing, dividing, dressing, assaying, debt
Doctor and club, clay and barber
Total £8.19.2
leaving 1/6 for two men for the month.

A tributer's fortune depended on his finding a rich lode of ore and on his knowledge and experience. A tutworker's depended on the difficulty of the job and the competition to do it; several workers competing against each other by offering to do more work for less money kept wages down. On average, Hamilton Jenkin calculates, a tributer earned £2.18.2 in a month and a tutworker £2.13.8.

Miners had to pay for candles, powder, fuse, shovels, clay, tramming. No wages were given until two months work had been done, and there was a fine for leaving deads (rocks) in the levels. Also the wages were counted on a '5-week month' which seems to mean for 48 weeks in a year.

On the surface there were men minding engines, fires, kibbles and stamps, and carpenters, masons and smiths, and there were women and children breaking the ore, discarding the worthless stones, washing the ore with water before sending it to the stamps to be crushed to gravel. It was then shaken with water in buddles until ready for smelting. You can see the whole process at Blue Hills Mine, St Agnes. Children aged 8 earned 2d or 3d per day at this. The hardest task was stooping to sieve copper ore in water. They worked a ten-hour day in summer and from dawn to dusk in winter, and sometimes twice as long. Before each shift they might walk from Carnon Downs to Poldice, Clifford United or Chacewater and afterwards home again. Girls and women, balmaidens, earned 9d per day hitting lumps of ore with hammers, and then copper ore on an anvil, on open hillsides or in a draughty shed. At Dolcoath an oven was provided and hot water (Lady Basset again?) and they brought what food they could.

'They have a great dislike to agricultural work' wrote the Commissioners of 1864, mining being better paid and the hours shorter.

George Henwood wrote of Cornish miners in 1855:

'Their recklessness will be difficut to overcome. Exposed as they are to momentary destruction from premature blasts, falling from ladders, crumbling of earthwork, irruptions of water and falling of rock, they evince a heedlessness truly unaccountable, nor can the remonstrances or threats of captains prevent the evil. They will seldom keep the ladders in proper repair unless compelled. I have seen a man sitting on a powder barrel smoking a pipe and a candle merely stuck against the wall by a bit of damp clay.'

From Hamilton Jenkin's book about Cornish miners:
'At 6 a.m., 2 p.m. and 10 p.m. men and boys converged to the clanging of bells, changed into stained shirt and trousers, hard hats with candles stuck on them, and a ration of candles hung from a button, and descended on the man engine. The time to finish was guessed by the number of candles burnt, but a tributer might work 2 8-hour cores at a stretch, time being his own. Miners picked and blasted rocks, rolled barrels of ore, filled kibbles, maintained pumps, supported levels with timbers ...

'At Poldice one night Lisha Billing failed to come up and the mine captain sent his son to seek him. Where Lisha had been working there was a rock fall and he had lost his candles. In the darkness he had wandered through old levels and ladders, and he was found at last on the edge of a shaft safe because he had crawled pushing a rock ahead and stopped when he heard it splash downwards 70 feet.'

Another miner at Poldice was sent to find out why the mine was filling with water and waded up to his chest in water that came from a sewer in St Day.

Better times to come in the 19th century

The fire engines of Boulton and Watt dewatered the mines and enabled the miners to descend deeper. William Murdoch was sent from Birmingham to set up engines and maintain them, but there was a shortage of engineers and boiler houses were wet and rusty and oily and smelly. By the 19th century Trevithick improved the efficiency of engines so that they used less coal, and Harveys of Hayle were making the boilers and other parts. Miners had a chance to attend evening classes, the hospital at Truro took the sick and wounded, and the Royal Polytechnic Society studied their needs.

Sir Charles Lemon wrote in 1839:
'The Cornish miner crawls to his work through passages so low and so narrow as would impede the ventilation. He works for 8 hours a day in

places in which he cannot stand upright and in which free use of his limbs and expansion of his chest are impossible. The number of men employed occasions a serious diminution of air in these places in which the breathing of the men and combustion of their candles deteriorate the little air they get which is further polluted by the explosions of gunpowder.'

Both Dr Barham and Mr Blee were writing long letters to the Royal Comwall Gazette, on 11th December 1840 and 3rd December 1841 for instance. 'With regard to the general subject of injurious agencies which operate on our miners and the means by which the evils may be abated, it is important that an enquriy accurate enough to lead to conclusions beyond the reach of cavil, should speedily be carried out.'

Dr Barham goes on to estimate that the population directly maintained by mines in Cornwall is 100,000 of whom 30,000 are working, half of those men, a quarter boys under 18 and 6000 female. He has figures for the value of exported copper, tin and arsenic, and for the expenses of the adventurers, and goes on to show that accidents cause 1/5 of miners' deaths, while many deaths result from a slow kind of consumption peculiar to miners. This is his great contribution because he proves that miners are disabled in their thirties and forties by lung disease which possibly could be prevented. He found that about 150 boys under 13 work in Cornish mines and stated what seems obvious, that children need air and light and unconfined exercise.

He studied the ventilation, which early in the century was judged by whether a candle stayed alight. Some mines were 500 fathoms deep with tunnels hundreds of fathoms long at several levels, and the only air coming in from the vertical shaft. At the ends of the tunnels the air contained less than a quarter as much oxygen as fresh air, and too much carbon dioxide and gunpowder and candle smoke. The temperature may be 80° F and increased by the heat of men and explosions. Before work and after the miners climb down and up a series of 60-feet slippery ladders from and to the surface.

He proposed life-saving improvements:

No level should be less that 6 feet high and 3 feet wide.

The slope of ladders should be at least 18 inches per fathom and staves should be less than 10 inches apart.

Miners should have a route from shaft to changing house without needing to go out of doors and the changing house should be warm and dry and provided with hot water,

Each miner should be given a hot nutritious drink at the end of the core (shift). Lady Basset set the example at Dolcoath.

Each miner should be paid separately. Teams of miners were paid as a group and used to repair to the ale house to divide the money.

There should be machinery to raise men up the shaft.

All the levels should be ventilated with out-door air.

Accidents, mainly falls from ladders, falls of rock, premature explosions, kill too many miners, especially the young, and must be prevented.

From that time there were improvements:

Trevithick improved on Boulton and Watt's engines so that they did more work for less coal, and more engines in mines opened up deeper levels and employed more miners. Bickford's safety fuse allowed blasting from a distance, and Michael Loam designed a man engine, first used at Tresavean, to raise men from the depths. Engine houses, being more efficient, were cleaner, engineers learnt to service them, and mine lords with their high profits took more care with their men.

Tramlines were gradually introduced so that boys aged 9-12 years who generally pushed barrows through rock and mud were relieved of toil. Commissioners in 1842 wrote ' there is consideration on the part of the men of the age and powers of the young and a disposition to relieve them from excess of toil', especially as often fathers brought their sons to work with them.

Chemical Works

Upriver from Devoran chemical industries were crowded on the shores while men turned the mud searching for tin. On the Perranwell side there was a series of copper precipitating tanks, shown on a map of 1880. Copper salts are more soluble in water than tin salts and so more difficult to retrieve. Maybe in these tanks, by adding iron, copper sulphate could be split into copper and sulphuric acid, and the latter would go to the vitriol works at the bottom of Old Carnon Hill.

There were more chemical works at Bissoe: Conn's vitriol and manure works between Bissoe and Nangiles started before 1850; Todd's Arsenic Refinery and Cornwall Arsenic Works were active from about 1830 to 1930; there were ochre pits, an iron foundry managed by William Henry Tregoning, and a tin smelter. It was the industrial age and farming had no chance in the Carnon valley.

Previously allowed to rise through smelting house chimneys to be blown by the wind and deposited and accumulated on the ground killing vegetation and insects, in about 1840 arsenic found some uses. Mainly it was in demand in the United States to kill the boll weevil that ate cotton plants. Among the Gwennap and Poldice mines there are still to be found plentiful goldlike rocks which are iron and arsenic sulphides or mispickel. These were burnt with charcoal in calciners from which smoke was sucked through a maze of tunnels (lambreth) and out from a tall square chimney. As it passed a grey powder was deposited on the inside of the tunnels and when cool was scraped and collected by boys. More burning turns the grey powder into white crystals of arsenic oxide which used to be freely sold. Compounds of it were used as a medicine, as sheep dip, insecticide and in green paint. It is however incurably poisonous either quickly or over many years. Remains of arsenic works are still at Bissoe, Wheal Busy and Poldice.

Smelting

Broken rocks containing copper, tin, lead, have to be burned to release the pure metal from its oxides, in the case of tin to turn black tin to white, a process still to be seen at Blue Hills, Trevellas Coombe, St Agnes. Copper ore was sent to Wales or Liverpool to be smelted because it needed so much coal. Tin and lead were smelted in Truro and along the Carnon river, requiring coals, clay, lime and sand to be carried from the quays. Hamilton Jenkin describes smelting: finely broken tin ore was heated on a fierce coal fire, the molten rock was run into stone moulds, heated again and run into a basin. The workers stood in their leather aprons and watched as a block of applewood was dropped into the basin from a height whereupon the tin rose like a fountain and boiled 'with volcanic fury', bright sparks of hot metal flying around them. Finally the tin was poured into moulds containing 3 cwt and stamped with the smelting house symbol.

Truro had 3 smelting houses, at Carvedras, Tregolls and Newham. The Calenick one was built by Moult, the German who had engineered smelting by coal, in 1703. Closer to Carnon Downs were houses at Penpol and Bissoe. The Penpol one from 1827 to 1880 smelted lead in 8 furnaces, employed nearly 100 people producing 200 tons of lead in a month and sometimes ½ ton of silver. It was succeeded by a tin smelting house described for Viv Acton by Reg Crocker. Four square furnaces were lined by clay brought by horse tram. He helped his father load the tin ore, like brown sand, into a furnace. The hole was stopped by clay while the furnace was heated. When the ore had melted a long iron rod with a square end was rammed in and turned to break through the clay bungs on each side to let the molten ore flow out into a large container. It was then poured into moulds where the Lamb and Flag stamps were floated on top. Read Viv Acton's *Life by the Fal*.

Engineering

The south bank of the Kennal river at Perranarworthal was industrial too. Perran foundry was built by George Croker Fox and Robert Were Fox in 1791 and cast beams for mine engines, the only big foundry besides Hayle in west Cornwall. Perranwharf was less used after 1820, and Devoran bridge and the main road through Perranarworthal were built in about 1830, so road transport for giant iron machinery replaced sea transport. In 1840s the foundry made pumping engines for United Mines and for Tresavean and engines for draining Holland. 400 men were employed in 1860 but by 1879 the foundry closed.

Gunpowder

At Cosawes, where there is now a mobile home park, the manufacture of gunpowder from sulphur, charcoal and sodium nitrate started in 1809, and at Kennal Vale in Ponsanooth in 1812.

ELEVATION OF PUMPING ENGINE.

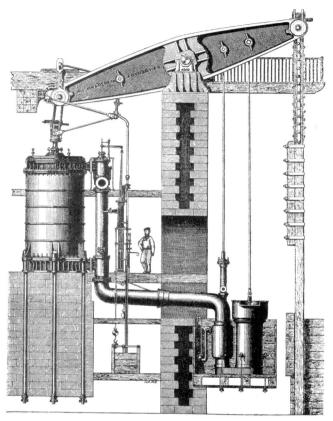

BUILT FOR ST. DAY UNITED MINES.

From the Perran Foundry catalogue of 1870

"The engine made by us for St Day United Mining Company (now called the Poldice Mines) is a good example of the Cornish engine as at present made, and gives a satisfactory idea of the general proportion of these Engines. It has been working under a load of 126,000 lb for the past eight years, and during the winter time has been kept continuously at work for six months, at an average rate of nearly eight strokes per minute, doing its work to the satisfaction of all concerned."

The Kennal river, tumbling down steep rocks, powered water wheels which turned machinery at 18 mills and ground the ingredients between millstones. The powder was shaken, compressed and dried and carried to the mines. One worker there from the age of 11 was Frederick Hamilton Davey, 1868-1915, who lived on Silver Hill Perranwell and wrote a book of his observations on flowers.

The transport and storage of gunpowder in mining areas was risky, because a spark or vigorous agitation could explode it. A spot in Carnon Downs was proposed in 1849 as a powder magazine, and the population within danger distance was counted. The site was in the triangle of fields between the bottom of Old Carnon Hill and Cobblers' Lane, which runs south from Wellington Place, and the tenants were Edmund Buzza and Thomas Martin. Within 300 yards to the north towards Carnon Wollas lived 5 families with between them at least 20 children. North-east were Upper and Lower Clydia, and Middle Devoran at 700 yards with 14 families and some cottages; to the south-east were 13 people in two houses, Emma Nichols' public house, and the railway weighing offices.

The field is now part of North Grange, in 1842 on a junction of Agar and Falmouth land. (See the map on page 86.)

Redruth and Chasewater Railway 1824-1915

Together with Devoran dock the railway employed about 20 Carnon Downs men in 1841, as agents, coal meter, porters, pilot, carrier, waggon driver, coal porter, not counting unspecified labourers. In 1861 there were 40 male railway employees listed in Carnon Downs census, and a girl of 15 keeping a gate, and there were lightermen and other watermen. Granite setts for the railway chairs are still visible between Twelveheads and Bissoe. See D.B. Barton's book *The Redruth and Chasewater Railway*.

Cornwall Railway

The branch line to Falmouth from Truro was built by 1863, and included eight viaducts, each one on masonry piers 22 yards apart and spanned by timber arches, pieces of which could I suppose be replaced as necessary. The line passes through Sparnock tunnel, over a bridge above

"Smelter", one of the Redruth & Chasewater Railway's three locos

Higher Carnon, over an embankment across the valley below Ringwell leaving a circular brick arch for the river, over a bridge on Ringwell hill, and across the viaduct to Perranwell Station. The viaduct crossed high above the Carnon river which was marshy and widespread, and the Redruth & Chasewater railway close to Catervilla or Keatrevilla. The timber structure was replaced by stone on new pillars in 1932.

304 miles and 11½ chains from Paddington

Occupations in 1871

By 1871 there were only 6 miners, and a variety of other occupations were followed from the age of 12 years upwards:

labourers	30
female housekeepers and servants	43
agricultural labourers and farmer's boy	24
farmers	12
female dressmakersand seamstresses	14
vitriol labourers and one manufacturer	7
miners and tinminers	6
tindressers and smelter, lead smelter	6
porters on quay	7
woodmen and sawyers	12
waterman, bargemen, boatman, master mariner	10
shoemakers	4
grocers and assistant, shopkeeper	7
male servants	3
butcher	3
porter, carrier, waggoner	10
carpenter	2
blacksmiths and apprentice	3
railway labourer, brakeman, engine driver, stoker, apprentice to engine fitter	5
thatcher and pig butcher, dairymaid, yeoman, groom	4
breaking mundic (aged 11 and 12), highway assistant, builder, road labourer, mason, undertaker	8
collector of poor rate, teacher, pupil teacher (age 13)	3
wheelwright, tramp, merchant, watchmaker	4
copper precipitator, sulphur burner	2

In Carnon Downs in 1871 there were 136 households containing about 617 people. Of these 248 were children aged 14 and less, of whom 139, aged 3 and over, went to school. There were church schools at Feock and

(Continues on page 177.)

Chiverton   (Photo John Crowe)

Trevince, guarded by goose 22 years old (Photo John Crowe)

Trevince: runner beans in June

Trevince Cottages in 2004 (Photo John Crowe)

Trough at Quenchwell (Photo John Crowe)

Samaria (Photo John Crowe)

Quenchwell, unfailing water supply

Satya

Wellington Place

Wellington Place barn

Tresithick to Penpol Farm (B.R. 21)

Lower Tresithick

Higher Tresithick

The Cottage, Tresithick

Old Barn, Chyreen Lane

Chyreen

Algarnick Farmhouse

Killiganoon

Tregye

Coalbrookdale cast iron pot (Photo John Crowe)

Slate meat safe and dolly tub   (Both photos John Crowe)

Cloam oven and spit in Helston Museum

Thwacking cob

Chaffcutter

Seed drill in Helston Museum

David Griffiths' chaffcutter, plough and trough

Spare wheel

At Pill Farm:
Pikes
Bull lead
Hayrake
Shepherd's crook

Wooden wheelbarrow

Haygatherer at Pill Farm

Harrows at Pill
Farm

Farm tool shed

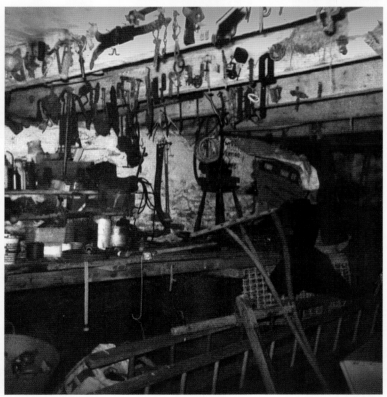

Devoran and Methodist Sunday Schools at Carnon Downs and Devoran. Please see Mrs Blunden's essay on local education in F.P.H. 1 and 2.

27 people were over 60, most of them still working; Edward Olive of Ebenezer and Loveday Gay of Caledgy were the only 80-year-olds.

A Brakesman Killed

'An accident, attended by fatal consequences, occurred on Thursday on the Redruth and Devoran Mineral Railway where it crosses the road leading from Carnon Downs ... to Perranwell. The railway, which is old and now but little used, belongs to Redruth and Chasewater Railway Company. Coal supplies for the mines on the south side of Carn Brea are conveyed from the little port of Devoran over it and from the mines are forwarded tin ore, arsenic etc for shipment at Devoran. The traffic however is so inconsiderable that never more than two trains run over the line in a day, and often only one. The usual speed of the train is 10 or 12 miles an hour. At noon yesterday the engine Spitfire was taking several trucks to Devoran. Three of the trucks were in front of the engine and seven behind, most being empty. Wiliam Francis the driver and E. Webber the stoker were on the engine, and Stephen Gay, a brakesman, was in the leading truck. When the level crossing just by the old vitriol works with the big stack was reached, the first truck was seen to jump violently and to leave the rails, the other two trucks with the engine following. As the engine was only travelling at the rate of ten miles an hour, and the brake was applied and the steam shut off at the first indication of mishap, it was but a very little while before the train was brought to a standstill. The two front trucks ran into the stone hedge which separates a narrow road running parallel to the line, and they were thrown lengthways across the railroad. This was just by the vitriol works where the metals run in a space about 18 feet wide between the stone hedge and a wall. In this narrow compass the trucks became tightly wedged and formed a barrier to the rest of the train. The 7 trucks behind the engine kept on the rails, and the engine was not damaged to any extent, but the foremost trucks were much splintered and broken.

'Gay was thrown out of the first truck, and the derailed portion of the train passed right over him. The men on the engine immediately went to

Stephen Gay stands on the back buffer of "Miner", another of the
Redruth & Chasewater Railway's locos

his assistance. Gay was in such an awkard position that they had to crawl
under the wreckage of the trucks and carry him from where he was lying
between the wheels of the engine. It was at once seen that he was badly
injured. Francis and Webber, who are both ambulance men, did what
they could in the way of first aid, and used a piece of broken wood from
the debris as a splint, when it was found that one of Gay's legs was broken.
The poor fellow was in agonies from severe internal injury, and a
conveyance was at once procured, on which he was taken to the Royal
Cornwall Infirmary, William Curnow, P.C. Bennett and J. Woolcock, who
recently passed examinations in the ambulance class organized by the
local Technical Education Committee, accompanying him.

'The cause of the accident seems quite clear. At the level crossing the
rails are slightly below the surface of the road, over which there is a deal
of heavy vehicular traffic. Owing to the recent spell of dry weather there
are patches of loose stone about, and the appearance of the crossing
would indicate that the men employed in keeping the road in good order
had put a certain amount of stone packing along by the rails to fill up
indentations. With this abundance of loose stones close to the railway it
would be easy for stones to lodge on the face of the metals. It was almost

obvious that an obstruction of this nature caused the trucks to jump the line. There is no reason to suspect any wilful or malicious act, but on the other hand it is highly probable that some of the carts engaged in conveying sand from the river close by displaced a quantity of the loose stone, and that this was deposited on the rails. The line in the vicinity of the accident is in a good state of repair. Two or three rails were forced out of position by the accident.

'Gay succumbed to his injuries last evening. He had sustained a compound fracture of the left leg, which limb was simply splintered, and in addition there were injuries of a fearfully painful nature at the lower part of the abdomen. The house surgeon at the infirmary and doctors Sharp and Carlyon did all in their power to alleviate his sufferings and save his life. Gay was conscious almost to the last. His home was in Carnon Downs. He was a widower about 35 years of age and leaves two children. His wife died but a short time ago.'

Other accounts mention that the crossing keeper was his sister-in-law, and that his father-in-law was the engine driver. The accident happened at the bottom of Old Carnon Hill and was reported as above in a newspaper of March 1899. It is locally believed that Stephen Gay's two little girls were brought up by relatives at Heath Farm.

News from *West Briton*

1817 'To be let ... farm called Come-to-good ... together with rope-walk thereon consisting of rope-house, hemp-loft, copper furnace, capstan, heads, jacks...'

1817 'The standard barrow for carrying copper ore contains 3 hundredweight, and allowing for the barrow and wetness the whole can be little less than 4 hundredweight. This burthen is borne by all manner of persons employed in dressing and weighing.'

1823 'A woman about 17 years of age met an untimely death by retiring to a stamp shed in Poldice mine, going too near the axle by which stamps are set in motion her clothes were caught and she was drawn in and crushed.'

1831 'Mr Robarts of Lanhydrock has given 39 stream tinners each a shirt made of blanketing.'

1833 'Two miners on their way from Miners Arms to St Day did not reach home. Their bodies were found at the bottom of an open shaft. Old Mineshafts abound in Gwennap.'

1833 'A lad about 15 years old working at Consolidated Mines fell from a ladder to a depth of 200 fathoms.'

1834 'Joseph Wolf, 11 years old, when proceeding to his home at Bissoe smelting works, the night being dark, walked into a pit filled with water into which smelters throw the hot metal. He was dreadfully scalded and died next day.'

1835 'James Davy, 21, kibble filler at Consolidated Mines, was descending on a chain, which some tributers had substituted for ladders. The chain slipped from the beam and he fell with it 7 fathoms and was killed.'

1838 'John Jose, in crossing the Redruth and Chasewater Railway at Consols counthouse was knocked down by a horse that was drawing a train of waggons.'

1840 'Dr Barham reports that conditions for children employed at Perran foundry compare well with other manufacturing districts.'

1847 'Young men connected with Perran foundry having formed a cricket club obtained permission to play in Sir Charles Lemon's park at Carclew.'

1849 'Miners as a class sacrifice their domestic comforts to their love of dress. Many who come out arrayed in flounces emerge from holes and dens resembling pigsties.'

1853 'Perran Wharf Mechanics Institution. The gardens of Carclew were thrown open through the kindness of Sir Charles Lemon, for the flora dance, tea on the grass, airs by Emidy's band, and healthful amusements on the lawn.'

1861 'John.Moyle, standing on a plat of the 140 fathom level at St Day United, had his leg caught with the chain of the fire whim by which he was drawn to the surface head down and escaped with little hurt.'

1862 'I once asked a miner what he most wished for on coming up from his work in the mine. "A dry shirt; we get into a sweat in walking to the mine, change our clothes, hang up our shirts wet with sweat, and so put 'em on when we come to grass".'

1865 'A marked change has taken place in the mining population. Small undertakings are being wound up, larger ones unprofitable, trade is falling off, credit is dearer, small traders suffer from debts suddenly made through customers emigrating.'

1866 'Unprecedented exodus of the bone and sinew of the working population of our county mainly to North America. Many hundreds find their way to Australia and New Zealand thereby relieving us of the surplus population of the mining districts.'

1867 'In a year 7,380 miners have left Cornwall, for America, Australia, New Zealand, California, Scotland and North England.'

1867 'A man having wife and 6 children should consume nearly a sack of flour per month. The price of a sack of flour was 30/- 2 years ago and is now 52/-. Miners' wages cannot provide enough.'

1868 'Fear of bread riots'

1868 'Great Wheal Busy abandoned, 600 hands thrown out of employment.'

1871 'Miners not allowed to earn 50/- per month for 2 successive months.'

1871 'In Carnon Valley precipitate works: scraps of iron in drains attract particles of copper which is scraped off.'

1871 2,750 persons from Chacewater, Gwennap and Redruth moved to north of England where they can earn 50/- per week, work regular hours sheltered from wet and cold, have simple duties, and everything orderly.'

1875 '10,576 emigrants from Cornwall to Australia in last 6 months.'

For more information:

Cornwall Record Office documents WH 1407 -1416, WH 2033 - 5,
        WH 1512, WH 5476, EN 1525, EN1313, EN 582, EN 97 - 8,
        AD 408, ST 1243, X 77/6, CY 3804.
Ask in Courtney Library Truro and in Cornish Studies Library Redruth
Royal Cornwall Gazette December 11 1844 page 4, and December 3
        1841, letters from Dr Barham
Royal Cornwall Polytechnic Society 1871, lecture by Robert Blee.
Dines British Geological Survey 1958
Hamilton Jenkin *The Cornish Miner*
Old Cornwall magazine Autumn 1994: Roy Woolcock on Bissoe
Viv Acton *Life by the Fal*
D.B. Barton *The Redruth and Chasewater Railway*
Barry Simpson *Devoran*
Bob Acton *The Landfall Book of the Poldice Valley*, and *Exploring
        Cornwall's Tramway Trails*
Bob Acton and Kenneth Brown *Exploring Cornish Mines*
West Briton: 19th century editions or extracts selected by R.M. Barton

ROADS THAT COME TOGETHER

Ten miles from
John Ogilby's
Plimouth to
Senan road map
1675

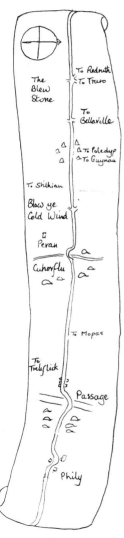

On Carnon Downs, a waste area with scattered settlements, roads met from many directions: from Perranwell and Penryn, from Gwennap and Redruth, from Bissoe and Baldhu, from Penweathers and Truro, from Porth Kea and Feock, from King Harry Passage and Restronguet, from Narabo and Point. It must have seen passing adventurers, engineers, rebels, armies, preachers, post-horses, laden mules, farmers and miners. Yet John Wesley in his travels on horseback through Cornwall noted that the inhabitants of the north-east had only a vague idea of towns and villages other than their own and could not direct him beyond their village.

Miss Philbrick of Algarnick Cottage and Tresithick Lane, having examined maps from 1660 onwards, wrote about Feock roads in a paper which is kept in Courtney Library. Maps can be found in both Courtney Library and C.R.O.

The oldest is John Ogilby's strip map of 1675 (C.R.O. AD 177/2). It is in the shape of a ribbon from Plymouth to Sennen. There are some recognisable place names and rivers, but the route is drawn straight and lacks the shapes of present day roads. From 'Passage from Phily' there are seven side turnings and a curve over a river at 'Cuhorflu'. From there to Redruth the road passes 'Blow ye Cold Wind' and turnings to Stithians, Guynan, PoleDyp, Penryn, Bellaville, and the 'Blewstone'. Passage to Cuhorflu and from there to Bellaville are each 4 miles, and from Cuhorflu to 'Blow ye Cold Wind' is ½ mile. 'Blow Cold Wind' is still a place name today. But where does the route cross the Carnon river? It could be at Bissoe Bridge, Dunstan's Ford or at the bottom of Old Carnon Hill.

Cornwall was the first county to be mapped at 1" to the mile. Joel Gascoyne, born in 1650, was a skilled chartmaker, engraver and surveyor, and was employed by Lord Robartes to survey his estates and then all of Cornwall, which took him 6 years. His 1699 map can be bought in folio edition and is decorated with drawings of his surveying instruments. His method is unknown but maybe he measured exact lengths of coastline and rivers and the angles in them, and filled in the rest by triangulation. It is printed in 12 parts each just under 1" to the mile. He has symbols for 'gentleman's seat', village, village with cottage, enclosed road, open road.

Gascoyne shows three crossings of the Carnon River: Old Carnon Hill or Lower Carnon, and Dunstan's Ford or Higher Carnon, both passing through Perranwell, and Bissoe Bridge which leads to 'Blow Cold Wind' and Lanner. Approaching Carnon Downs from the east are three roads, one passing Tregye, and two further north.

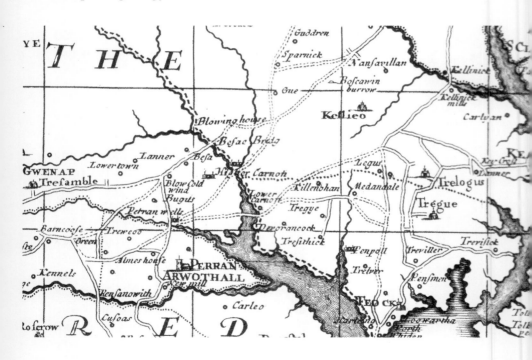

Part of Joel Gascoyne's 1699 map

UNWILLINGLY TO SCHOOL

'Few are desirous of the means of education.' In Feock parish 'two small schools exist, one containing 16 children taught by a woman and another with 10 children taught by a man.' (Rev. J Symons, Vicar, about 1815)

At that time the providers of schools were the National Society for the Education of the Poor in the Principles of the Established Church and the undenominational British and Foreign School Society. Both worked mainly in towns and taught up to 1000 children in one building by using the older children as teachers. When the National Society surveyed Feock in 1846 they reported one school in Feock with 22 pupils on weekdays and 19 on Sundays. They decided to build two new schools, one in Feock, one in Devoran.

For the Devoran school £245 was given by local subscription and £65 by the government. Income was £5 p.a. from a charity, £15 voluntary contributions, and £10 from daily pence collected from the children. The only teacher in the first 7 years, Miss Mary Towan, untrained, had 62 pupils, sometimes 92. Children brought their slate pencils, and I suppose lunch, and fires were lit 'when necessary' and when there was enough firewood.

There was a rival. The Wesley chapel opened a school in 1868 and had 110 pupils, the boys paying 6d per week, the girls 3d and infants 2d. The one teacher, Mr Fifoot, trained in Westminster, was paid £86 per year. The problem for the church school was that its grant depended on the number of pupils attending and it lost some pupils to the chapel. In Carnon Downs children had been attending Sunday school before 1825 at Ebenezer and after that date in the chapel.

There were also dame schools: above the stable of Carnon Downs chapel was one, and another was in the loft at Trerise, where children sometimes attended in the evening.

The 1841 census does not record school attendance. In 1851 88 children are recorded as scholars, out of a total of 244 children aged 14 and under. In 1871 there were 139 scholars aged 3 to 14, and one aged 18. At that time the slumps in mining and agriculture, and the emigration

Where public education
began in 1825

of neighbours, perhaps made the out-door labouring lives of their parents and grandparents less attractive, and spending their youth within stone walls, windows high above their heads, may have seemed necessary.

Attendance was the problem. The government grant depended on the number of children attending, and success in the annual examination. A child who attended less than 250 ½-day sessions in a year could not sit the examination and so brought in no grant. An attendance officer enquired after families who failed to attend but he could not make them come to school. There were good reasons for 'mitching', that is missing school: children were needed to pick stones in fields, to pick up potatoes, to act as weights on the coal scales on the quay, to fetch 'liver and bits' from market and pilchards from boats, and their fathers sometimes took them to sea. In 1888 children from Higher Devoran helped with the harvest, the men being unwilling. In winter non-attendance had to be excused because of epidemic infections and heavy snow. In 1888 the headmaster wrote, 'I have been informed that there are families not attending my school; ample scope for attendance officer if he desires to do his duty.' Dame schools continued to rankle; 'I hear that a dame school has been opened in Carnon Downs in a private house; two girls admitted have been attending the dame school and are consequently greatly behind in their work.' 'Some Carnon Downs children come to school at the age of 7 years perfectly ignorant and then attend irregularly. What can any teacher do?'

Lady Boscawen offered tea for any child attending 300 times in the year.

The 1870 Education Act said that elementary schools with qualified teachers should be provided for all, and the 1880 Act allowed that children could be compelled to attend.

Some of the lessons at Devoran

Children entered standard 1 at age 6 and by passing examinations progressed to standard 6. Here are some comments from the logbook from 1865 to 1890.

The first class wrote an account of Moses from memory on their slates.
The 2nd and 3rd standards can do as far as tens of thousands accurately.
A first attempt by 1st and 2nd classes to paraphrase poetry.
Exercise in composition, the subject being Minerals of England.
Lessons on digestion and the stork.
Taught standards IV and V rules of the metric system.
Rev Forrest visited and questioned the lower classes on the life of Noah.
Rev Gillan took New Testament lessons.
No play for the week, singing lessons instead.
Began to teach drill in leisure times.
Standards IV - VI are doing analysis of sentences and parsing. They don't seem to like Geography.
Pleased with French exercises by standard V1. Geometry well done by standards IV - VI.
Formed a class in algebra for elder boys. Gave standards VI and VII a lesson in Latin prefixes. Gave standard VII a lesson on stocks.
Standard III's knowledge of adverb and pronoun is limited. Verb is weak.
Upper standards know Latin, Greek and old English prefixes.
Drawing to be a class subject.
Geography is backwards. Boys of standard III must at once provide themselves with an atlas.

Lady Boscawen arranged for elder girls to attend cookery classes in public room Truro. She invited boys too, pointing out how useful cookery would be to men in the army and navy and to fishermen.

Infants

The noise made by the under 6s was a problem. They were supposed to learn to read, write and do sums. In 1882 nature, object lessons and manual tasks were recommended.

From the log book:

Louisa Woolcock and Ethelinda Opie, both aged 2, were admitted.
Owing to the noise made by very young children Mr Philpotts ordered that no more children under 4 are to be admitted.
Infants doing fairly well under Miss Pascoe. Object lessons a source of great pleasure. They have studied 'table', 'use of the hand', 'cotton', 'cow', 'window' and 'cat'.
Have let the infants into the yard during the afternoon to ventilate the room.

Discipline

Inspectors looked for good behaviour and discipline was expected of pupil teachers.

From the log book:

Pascoe, Pearce and Gibbon stayed away at play in the dinner time until 2.30 p.m. and received a flogging.
James Wilton is punished for playing truant for two days.
Bessie Cook and her two little brothers are expelled in consequence of the insult offered to the school by the removal by the parents of their brother from us.
Rev Tucker passing before the school hears an uproar within. He finds several boys attempting to throw down the door between school and closet. He finds that William Martin was the concocter of the scheme, and had discovered the law of the lever.
Children in the first three classes come an hour early for repetition of lessons.

Some boys suspected of stealing - short moral lesson. Five boys punished for bad conduct at church. Little girl of III class guilty of falsehood - moral lesson on truthfulness.

Rev Forrest cautioned children as to the manner the inhabitants intend to deal with those who wilfully destroy people's property.

Caught several boys smoking in the playground.

Was obliged to punish Jane Williams who showed great stubbornness to her teacher when warned against copying sums.

Punished Thomas Rowe for impudence and dismissed him from school.

George Williams, Joseph Moab, Matthew Warren and Joseph Dunstan met a poor old man at the vitriol works and severely stoned him. The case being taken in hand by the policeman and some of them having been punished by their parents, I only cautioned them.

Edward M was punished for obtaining money by fraud from a captain and telling lies. P.C. Oliver gave him a thrashing in the school.

Caned W Paull twice. Was obliged to cane several on account of incessant talking.

Forbade chewing pitch.

John Peters mitching. His mother sent a message for me to cane him. His mother sent another message not to cane him but to keep him in.

Mary Ann Sprague impertinent to me because I kept her in until 12.45. This afternoon I punished her with 4 strokes on the hand.

For continual bad behaviour I gave John Curtis and W Behenna several stripes an the breach.

Elizabeth Trethowan slow in obeying me so I gave her a few strokes on the shoulder.

Three Behennas left school. Mrs Behenna would not allow them to make a bow on entering and leaving school. I called them back and made them do it.

Caned Samuel T rather severely for being in a state of intoxication last Friday.

Teaching Children to Teach

Head teachers, all certificated, from 1863 to the end of the century were in turn Messrs Dennis, Walker, Phillips, Cook, Watson Fellowes, Hill, Henry, Samson, Daniell and Cock, and assistant mistresses were in turn Misses Pascoe and Yeoman, Mrs Hosking, Misses Sarah Penrose, Laura Webber, Rosine Cartrell and Chapman.

There were also pupil teachers, often pupils who had passed the standard VI examination at the age of 12 and stayed on. The head master taught them before and after school and they had to pass a pupil teacher examination in Falmouth.

From the log book:

The pupil teacher had charge of the school the whole week. He is active and obliging.

George Williams will be a pupil teacher.

I take the pupil teachers from 12-1.0 p.m.

Pupil teacher lessons commence before breakfast 6.45-7.45 a.m.

Pupil teachers of the third year: G Williams passed fairly and J Nichols must improve her composition. J Clear gave two moderate scripture lessons to standards I and II. He needs much greater control over his class. J Clear satisfies requirements of Honours certificate.

Anna Maria Martin acts as monitor. She absented herself entirely from her duties because she cannot submit herself to the master's will.

H A Clear has obtained second division in Bishop's Prayer Book prize list being 28th out of 122 candidates.

T Mitchell works actively with me in the evenings preparing for the examination. He is again behind with his Euclid.

The French of the pupil teachers was creditably done.

Money

1864 Rev Tucker ordered new sets of reading books.

1862 Unless there is marked improvement in arithmetic the grant will be reduced.

1869 Fresh supply of slates

1873 Tin pitchers having been procured the children are supplied with water and a basin. Towels have been procured for the girls.

1876 Introduced new harmonium for school, cost £7.7.0

1880 Grant received £112.11.0

1866 November 20 fire lighted for the first time this winter

1869 December 17 no fire today for lack of wood

1891 Free Education Act comes into force today.

1872 Instruction is unsatisfactory. Arithmetic is weak throughout the school, writing and spelling in the 1st and 2nd standard, and reading in the 1st standard. A great improvement must be made. One tenth of the grant has been deducted for defective instruction.

1887 Discipline is very good and the scholars have passed another most successful examination in all subjects. The paper work in particular is very neat, handwriting and spelling decidedly good and composition except for a few local colloquialisms sensibly and well expressed. The class subjects are equally satisfactory, the map drawings and exercises in grammar attain a standard of exceptional excellence.

1892 170 children present at Diocesan inspection, class excellent for 10th time in succession.

Information about schools came mainly from Devoran School logbooks held in C.R.O.; also from M A Blunden's notes which she kindly lent me. She wrote two articles in F.P.H.

News from the *West Briton*

1848 'J. Gilbert of Trelissick gave a teatreat to the children of all the schools in Feock, nearly 500.'

1855 'In mines in the parish of Gwennap 18 out of 40 children could not read or write.'

1855 Feock National School Treat. 'Time appointed for meeting 2.30 p.m. Feock children assembled at the church. Mrs Gilbert provided conveyance for the little ones. The children of Devoran having a long walk on a hot day were a little late so it was nearly 3.0 before all were assembled in the church. Short service (litany, thanksgiving read by vicar and address by Rev. Courtley not too long and most appropriate, 100th psalm sung). Children, over 200, walked to Porthgwidden. Tea provided in the garden, girls on upper and boys on lower terrace. Then to adjoining meadow to play until dusk. National anthem sung and cheers for queen and vicar.'

1864 'In mining districts one person in 24 persons goes to school.'

Joseph Locke, Blacksmith
Photograph from Arthur Mitchell

GOVERNING CLASSES

Taking care of the parish in the 19th century

Rates had to be collected for the upkeep both of the poor and of the roads. William Gerrish was appointed constable, and Edward Olive was to call on those who failed to pay. Walter Hearle was churchwarden and in turn members of the vestry were waywardens.

In 1845:
'5 people to be excused paying.'
'3 people are not maintaining their mothers.'
'Road to Ringwell must be repaired.'
'Paupers born in other parishes must be referred.'
'Ann Woolcock of Kea to be removed.'

In 1849 to 1913:
Poor rate is 1/- in £ and highway rate 6d.
'£10 to be given to Bridget Clyma for passage of her and her son to Australia.'
'Overseers of Battersea have ordered the removal of Tabitha Bray and 4 children and we object'.
'Charles Manuel the younger to be compelled to maintain his father.'
Edward Olive resigned in 1871 after 47 years in vestry.
'Vicar needs money for 2 schools.' Therefore extra 4d in £ to be collected.
22 people failed to pay the rates.
'Mary Gay to receive relief if she can find a clean house.' (P64/18/1)

At the end of the century rateable values dropped. Also tractors and motor traffic were increasing the cost of road maintenance. It was agreed not to spend parish money on coronation celebrations.

In 1913 Devoran school was taken over by the County council. Parents were urged to send children to school because the grant depended on numbers of pupils. At the same date it was decided that children in the workhouse (Union) should be kept separately from the elderly. (P64/8/1)

Miniature government

By 1894 the civil parish of Feock was the concern of representatives of the residents, namely William Woolcock, John Richard de Clare Boscawen of Tregye, and Samuel Williams of Higher Devoran. Early complaints were about water.

'At Chyreen cattle are in the habit of going to the well to drink and during heavy rains dirty surface water runs into it. 18 houses take water from it. Lord Falmouth has protected several wells but this one is in premises held from him.'

'Inhabitants at Carnon Gate complain that in winter a strong stream comes down the valley. The shute got covered over thus cutting off supply of drinking water.'
'Cover at Algarnick well being in a bad state leaves and dirt get into the water. Proposed that sanitary inspector should inspect.'
'Door required on Quenchwell well. Nothing done.'
'Wellington Place flooded.'
'Waste water is thrown in road at Carnon Gate causing stench.'
'Well at Carnon Gate contaminated by manure.'
Until waterpipes were laid in 1955 every householder depended on a well, usually shared, or a spring or stream.

Footpaths caused dispute:
'Tenants at Killiganoon complain of stopping up of path from farm to lodge.'
'Obstruction caused by gipsies' animals being tethered to hedges at Algarnick.'
'Licensed hawker to be asked to remove his mule further from the public road as he did not take much notice of the warning from the policeman.'
'Encroachment of a right of way by the putting up of a fence there.'
'Proposed road Point to Bissoe along railway.'
'Overhanging hedges at Gig Lane.'
'Road men constantly take away from Carnon Downs Green for repairing road.'
'Dangerous state of road through Gig Lane.'

It was still necessary to support the needy:

'Several old people had nothing but their pensions. They should be excused rates at the discretion of the overseer.'

'10 extra houses needed. No land available.'

'It is hard that poor people should have to go to Truro for a doctor.'

And education:

'Truro District Instruction Committee asks suggestions as to subjects. Proposed Fishing and Oyster culture.'

Parish collections for materials for sewing classes.'

Then came the 1914 war:

'Mr Langdon offers a house at Devoran for the Belgians.'

'Ask Ministry of Agriculture to explain allotments'...'means of increasing production of food'... 'spray potatoes.'

'The amount of sugar to be apportioned to growers of fruit for jam making.' (PC/FEO/1/1)

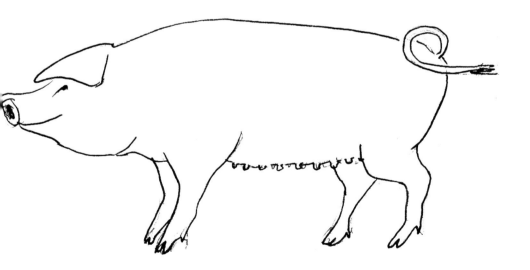

Key to the tithe map below
Scale c. 1:10000

LANDOWNERS

Green F — Earl of Falmouth
Yellow L — Sir Charles Lemon
Red A — Hon. Anna Maria Agar
E and MH — Elizabeth and Martha Hugo
Thomas Simmons

TENANTS

CT Charles Trengrove
DR Daniel Retallack
EB Elizabeth Burrows
EH Elizabeth Honeychurch
EO Edward Olive
GT George Tregaskis
HN Henry Nicholls
JC James Collins
JP Juliana Penrose
JT John Tregidgea
NT Nathaniel Trengrove

RCR Redruth &
    Chasewater Railway Co.
SM Stephen Martin
TM Thomas Michell
TP Thomas Pengelley
WDa William Daniel
WD William Dunstan
WG William Gerrish
WM William Murton
WS William Scoble
WT William Tallack